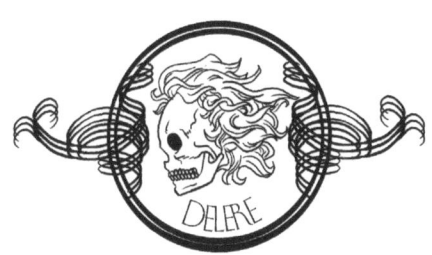

THIS PAPERBACK EDITION 1ST
PUBLISHED IN 2015 BY DELERE PRESS LLP

99 PROBLEMS TO BE TOLD TO A PLANT
& THE EXCAVATION OF ITS FUTURE
MEMORY © BERIT JANE SOLI-HOLT

FIRST PUBLISHED IN 2015 BY
DELERE PRESS LLP
BLOCK 370G ALEXANDRA ROAD
#09-09 SINGAPORE 159960
WWW.DELEREPRESS.COM
DELERE PRESS LLP REG NO. T11LL1061K

ALL RIGHTS RESERVED

ISBN 9789810972578

99 Problems to be told to a plant

&

The Excavation of Its Future Memory

by Berit Jane Soli-Holt

these pages are dedicated to
the one and always

Danielle Donelan

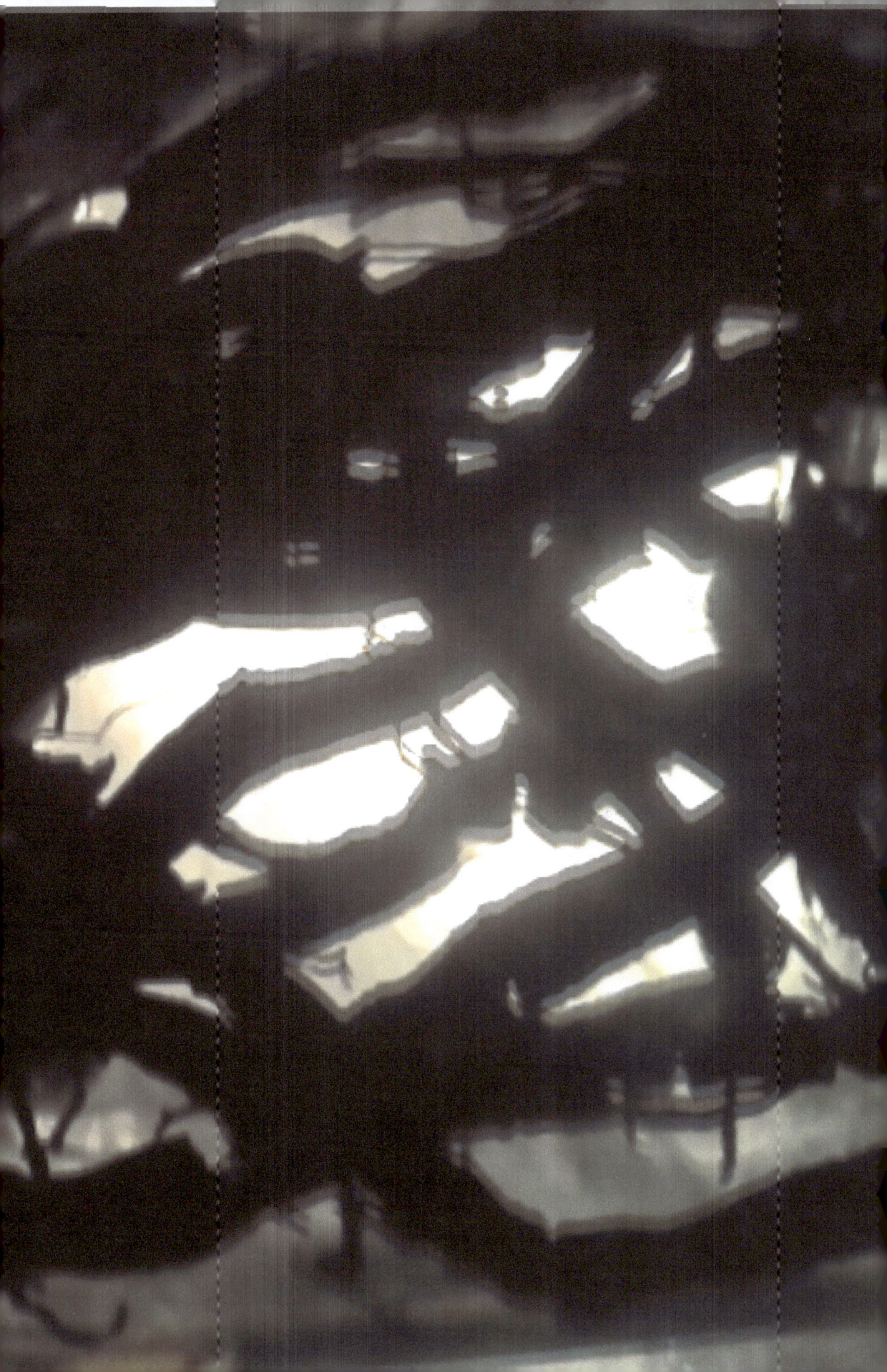

notes of an introductory sort

THE FIRST-ISH PART ENTITLED 99 PROBLEMS TO BE T[OLD] TO A PLANT WAS ENGENDERED BY ONE ROSEMARY LEE [IN] 2012 TO BE PRESENTED ALONGSIDE/WITHIN HER EXHIBITION FOR PANMEDIALE, ON SENSITIVITY, PLANTS & NOIS[E]

THE SECOND-ISH PART ENTITLED THE EXCAVATION[S] OF ITS FUTURE MEMORY (IN REFERENCE TO THE 99 PROBLEMS) IS EXACTLY THAT AND WAS COMPLE[TED] IN THE FALL OF 2014.

THE IMAGES WERE CAPTURED IN THE INTERIM PERIOD BETWEEN THE WRITTEN WORKS. THEY SERVE AS INVESTIGATIONS SOMETIMES SIMILAR IN NATURE TO THOSE WRITTEN IN A MORE EXPOSITORY FASHION.

THANKS TO DELERE PRESS
THANKS TO JEREMY FERNA[NDO]
THANKS TO YANYUN CHE[N]
THANKS TO ROSEMARY LEE
ALSO
THANKS TO YOU

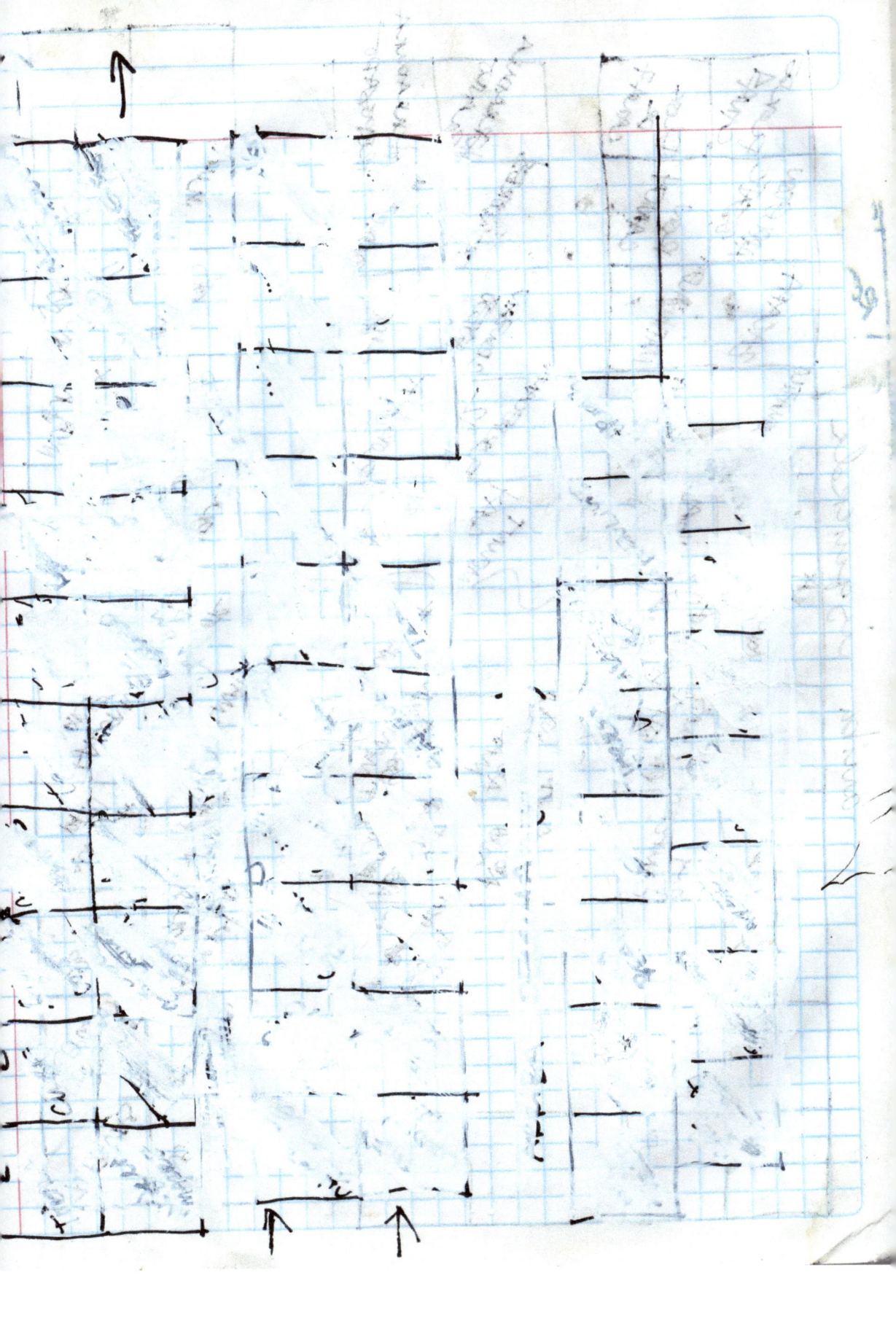

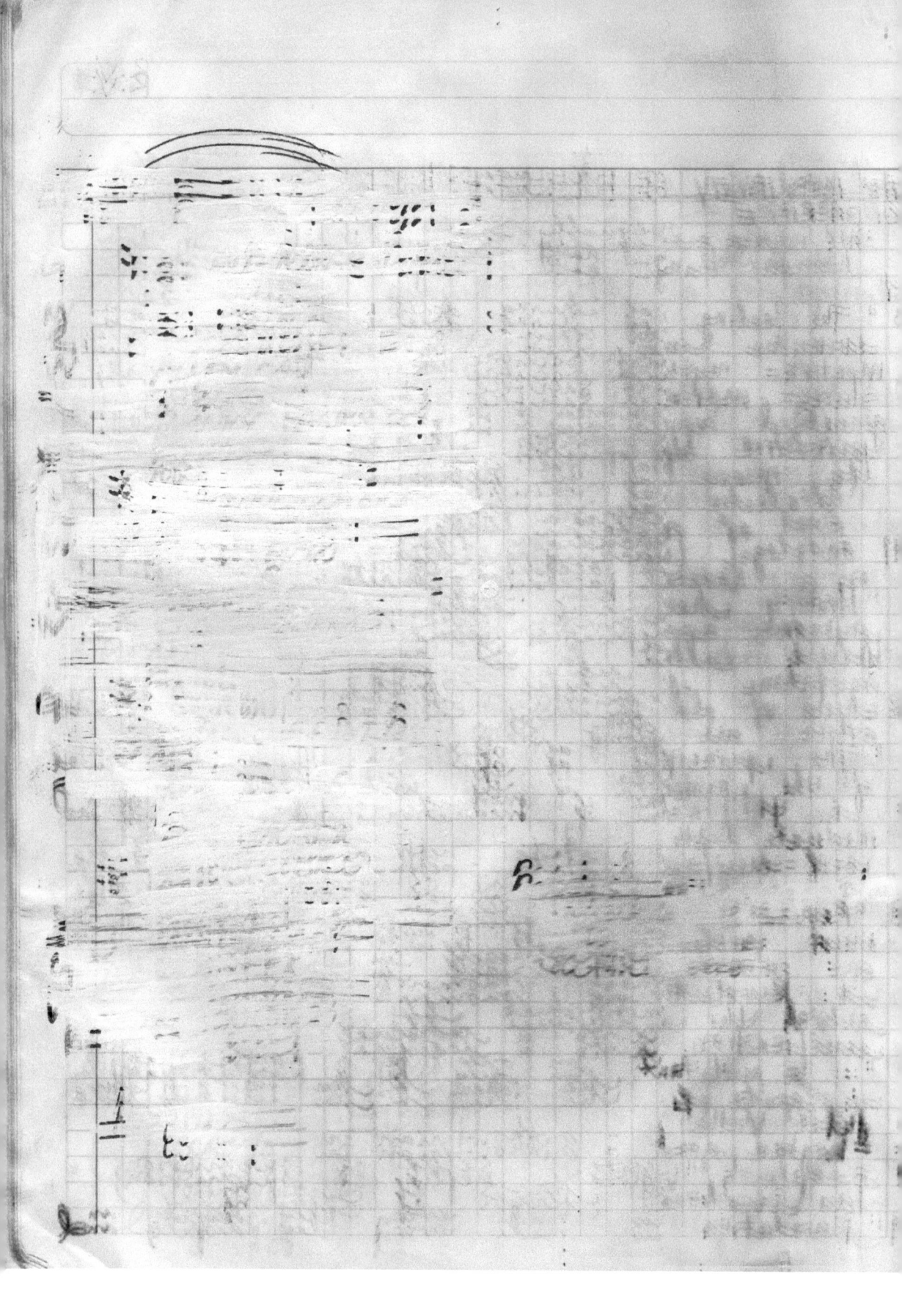

As for how to read this, well,

There is a schematic outlining how the aphorisms follow each other on the last page of the 99 problems. The numbers following after the first thirteen reflect the conceptual sequence or sequence of the base of the first thirteen. The list of the random order was created to be of use in performance, so nevermind that.

The excavation of its future memory has page numbers which the author does find a particular potency in reading in order. However, the text is printed not in the order of its conceptual lineage but in the order of its material order.

Oh yeah, there's an index that may prove useful as well, it is somewhere in the middle of the excavation. (An index of those sequences in the 99 problems.)

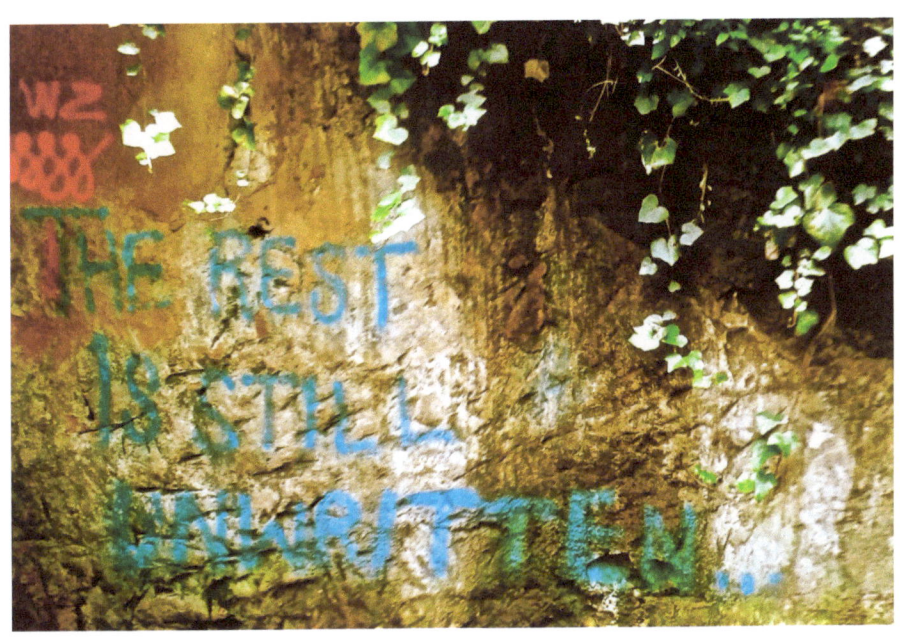

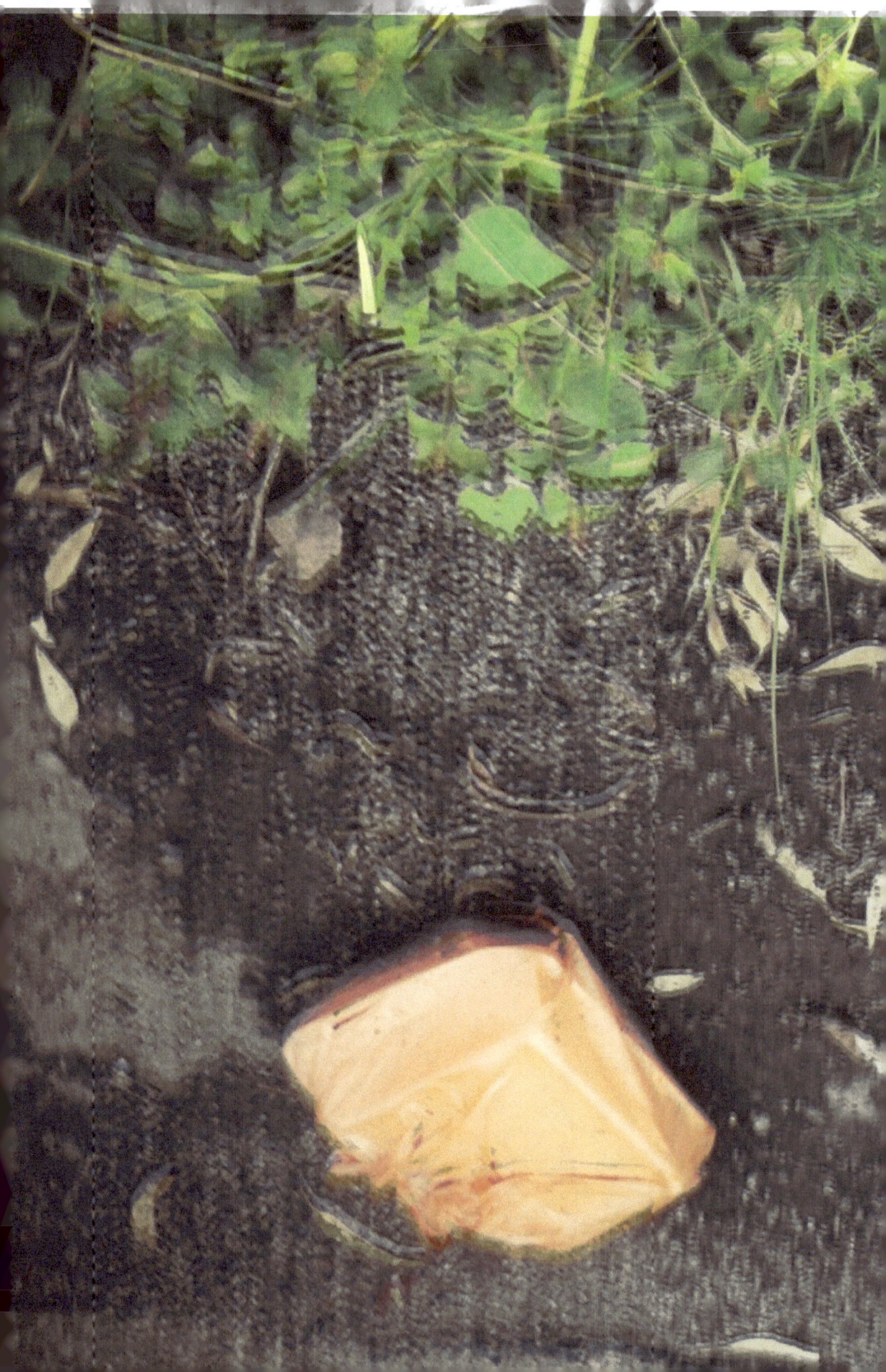

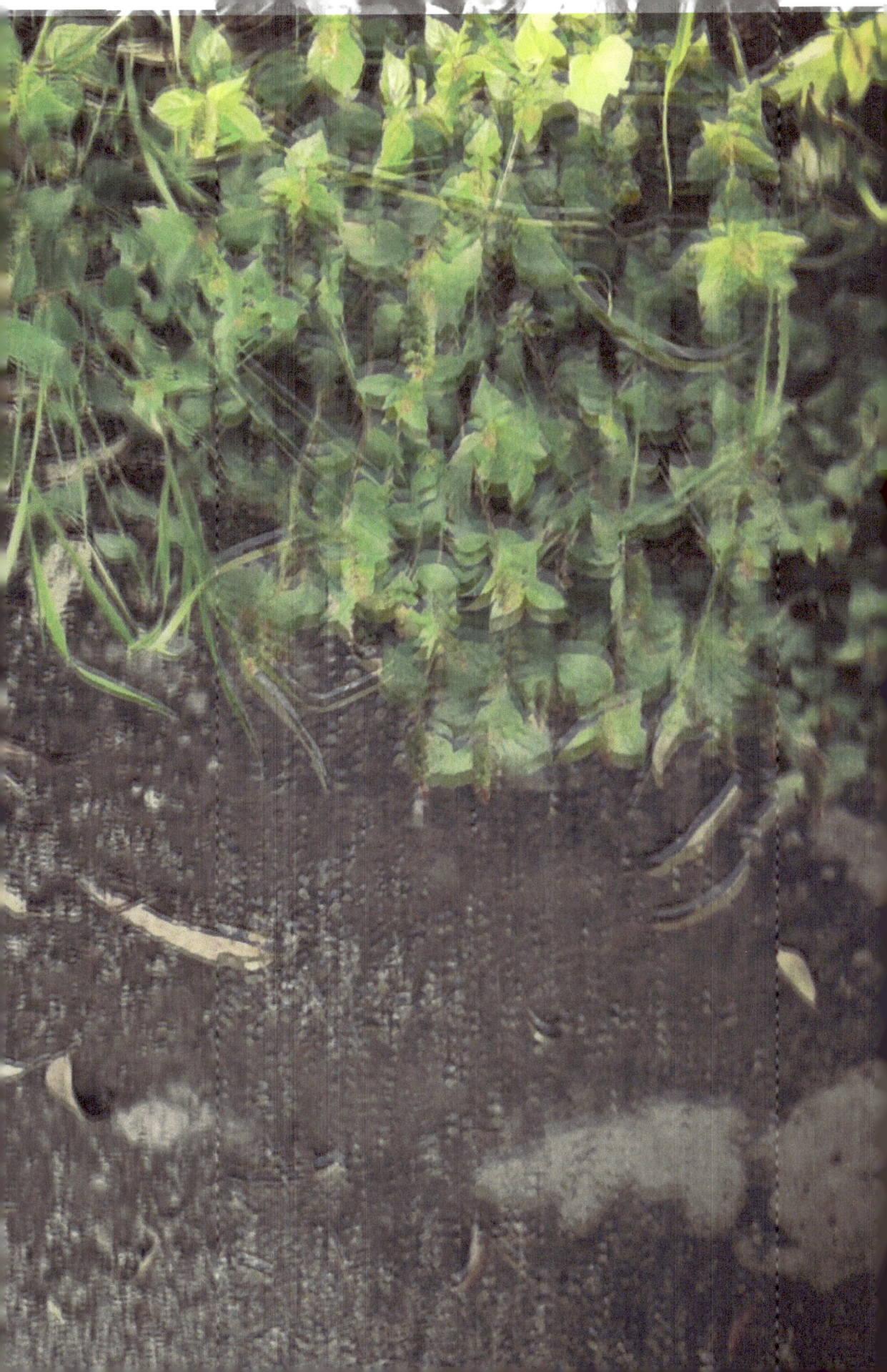

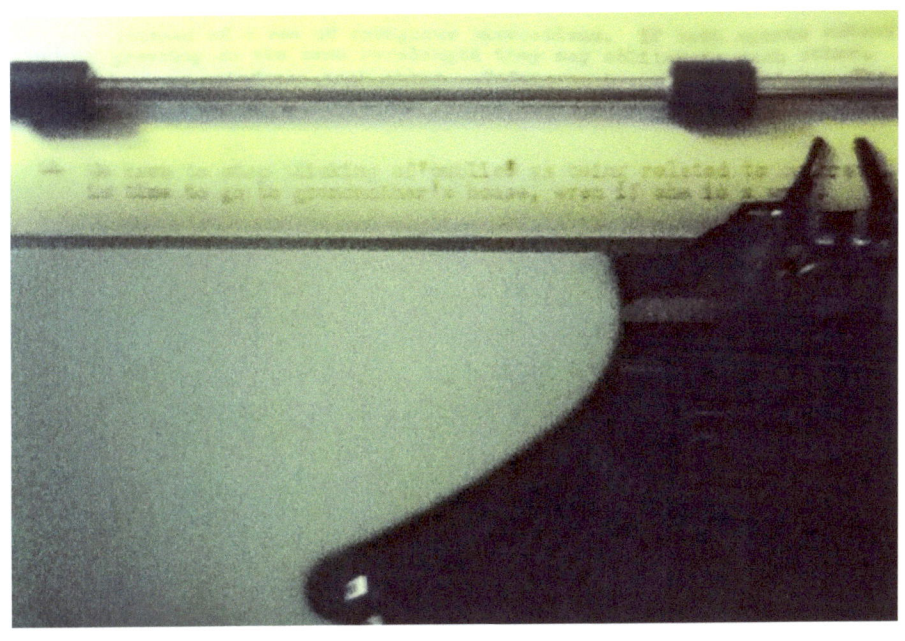

99 Problems to be told to a plant::

1 ~~[redacted]~~

2 A reaction: movement corresponding to an action of an agent in which the action remains under alien weather conditions, however, happens somewhere else under alien weather conditions.

3 ~~[redacted]~~

4 In consideration of the question: where does the grass meet the ground? There is the distinction=grass,and ground. supposing that all else through what appears to be the area at ground. Upon empirical restoration it becomes ground. This is still relient at absorbing islet. The question of hasting the empiries to gestionand the pixelization of the language while interested by question of the pixelization of the perceived called into pieces by words.

5 In consideration of the question: where does the grass meet the ground? What is a meeting? How does it work?

6 From Aristotle's "Problems," Book VII - Problems Arising from Sympathy, NUMBER 4: why do those who come to the aid of persons infected with certain diseases sometimes become healthy from contact with health? Is it because disease is motion, whereas health is rest? Therefore, the one wearily, the other do so tabily? Or is it because the one alone differs involuntarily, the other voluntarily? And what is involuntary differs from that is voluntary and what is due to forethought.

7 Briefcases that blow off the end of our arms like the white fluff of a dandelion.
   Briefcases that get stuck in animal fur like a burr.
   Briefcases that have to be ingested, digested, and excreted.

8 It isn't so much the inquiry into whether or not plants have emotions or senses, or capable of offspring et cetera and should be inquiry into the sensitivity of producing alkaloids and how they distribute them amongst themselves.

9 Light, sunlight, is crucial for the growth and development of herbs. But when dried and stored for human use, the qualities sought after in the herb diminish greatly when exposed to sunlight.

10   Can an interrogator force a confession from a chair?

11   The 'cult of values' as addressed by Theodor Adorno in his 12th lecture on the 'Problems of Moral Philosophy,' 9 July 1963:
  This cult arises then essentially from the yearning for guidance; its norms are justified not by reason but are themselves the product of yearning. This is not expressed in the values themselves. On the one hand, they are arbitrary; on the other, they express the weakness of human beings who are unable truly to determine themselves and to obey their own law, but who instead go in search of something that 'might come ~~and~~ by and take them along'. They pride themselves on the result which they refer to as 'solid' and 'down to earth'.

12   There exists no interface between grass & ground.

13   Is there a meeting between myself and "that which" comes by and takes me along"? In what neighborhood does that take place?

14   Vocalizing a set of problems to a plant asks the question of the intended listener. If the listener is not the intended listener, does the intention still act as movement although it becomes articulated through a foreign body?

15   A public of unintended listeners.

16   Generally speaking, a reaction is a movement in reverse while a response entails a reply. In some definitions a reply is reliant on language, while in others an action is sufficient even though this action does seem to require a reaching, meeting of the agent of initial action. A meeting does not appear to be integral in the motions of reaction.

17   To redact means to put into an appropriate form, to frame. ~~[redacted]~~. By making a place where nothing is there, redactions make suitable.

18   Responses are often redacted in printed interviews when the recorded response is not consistent with the interior logic of the question. This reaction, instead of containing within its grasp a projection of internal consistency, merely makes fresh event horizons to eat meaning.

19   We must put aside ~~[redacted]~~ sometimes.
       LANGUAGE

20   We encounter concepts by touch, not sight. Sight creates surfaces we anticipate touching; concepts are held before they can be seen. Concepts are felt. ~~[redacted]~~ To see a concept is to see interpretation already.

21   Mining our perception, we polish our words and hone our pixels.

22   The technology of meeting is photography. At which instant does a stem become a root? Can we capture it by name? When the space between meetings stretches out to reflect upon itself, we have cinema.

23   ~~[redacted]~~ however arbitrarily they are chosen, intentionally

24   Are movements only singularities? No. But metaphors seem to remain individual magic under the climate we find ourselves within.

25   The doctor that heals herself.

26   When we collect enough stuff to make a pile of meaningful things, the tendency is to render the pile invisible, thus redacting a portion of our environment. What grows there is feral.

27   Dinners are comprehensive files on time, place and companionship. Our movements amongst them dictate what documents become hardware and what remains software.

28   The misconception can easily become that plants are a minority. This is a grave misunderstanding.

29   It is not our cell walls that give us structure, but the communications between the cells. This by no means [account] we are any less rigid. The rigidity of our communicative properties creates structure, but the flow, the fluidity of exchanges and transport must be 'taken along' for the ride.

30   What do you want from me?

31   From "Herb Gardening for the Midwest" by Debra Knapke & Laura Peters:
   Pg. 31
   Fill a pot or planting tray to about 1" from the top with perlite, vermiculite or seeding soil mix. Moisten the soil and let the excess water drain away. Lay the rhizome pieces flat on the top of the soil and almost cover them with more soil mix. If you leave a small bit of of the top exposed to the light it will encourage the shoots to sprout. The soil mix does not have to be kept wet, but you should moisten it when it dries out to avoid having your rhizome rot. Once your cuttings have established themselves they can be potted individually and grow on in the same manner as the stem cuttings (see p. 28).

32   A confession is nothing more than a reaction. It is true that mechanical operations give us pleasure and that declaring our edges gives rise to sites of sensation. However, in revealing how we've grasped ourselves, how we've fought to inform our curves, we trick ourselves into thinking we've minimized a palpable distance. All we've done, in fact, is to render the distance senseless.

(3)

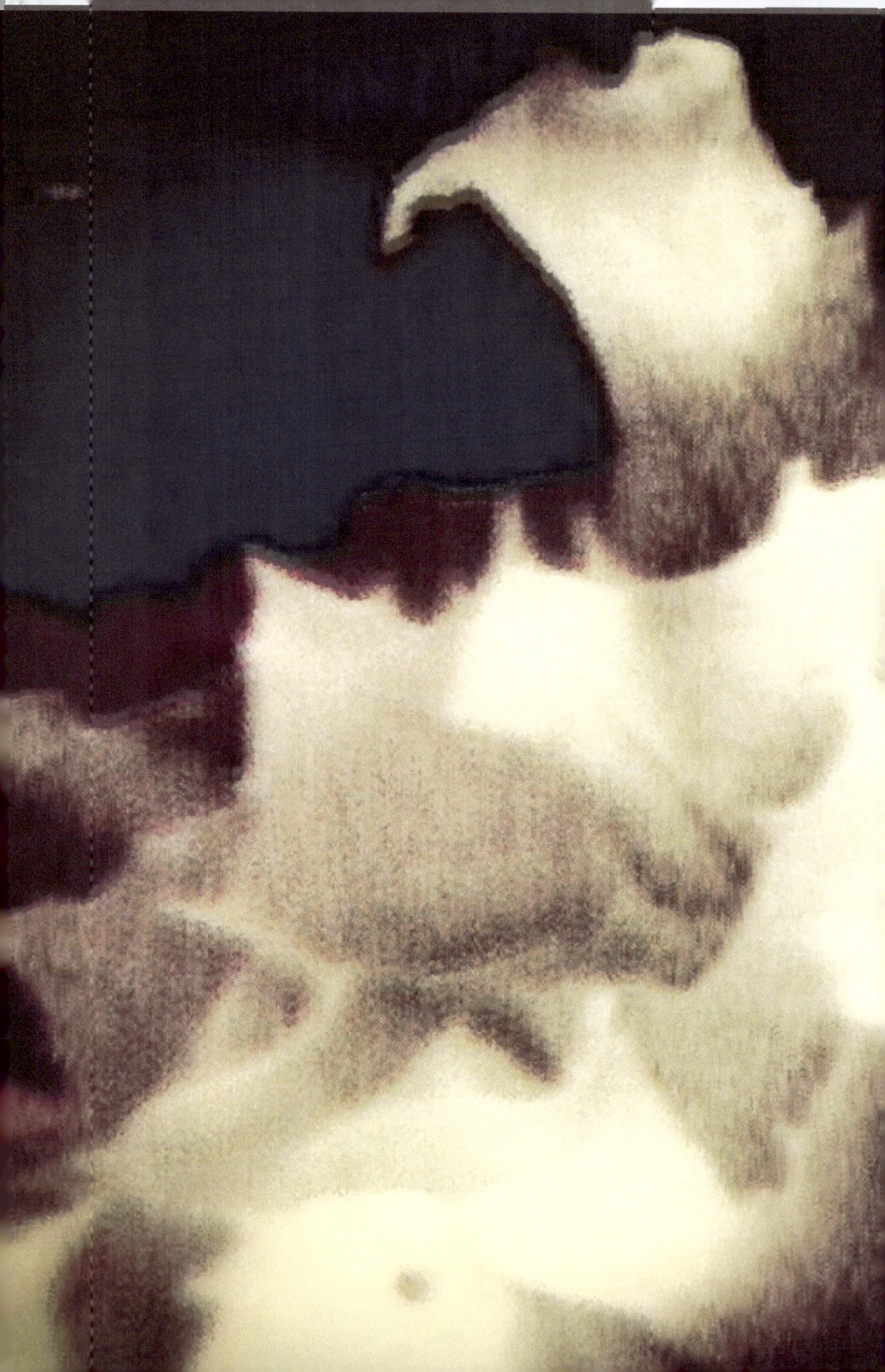

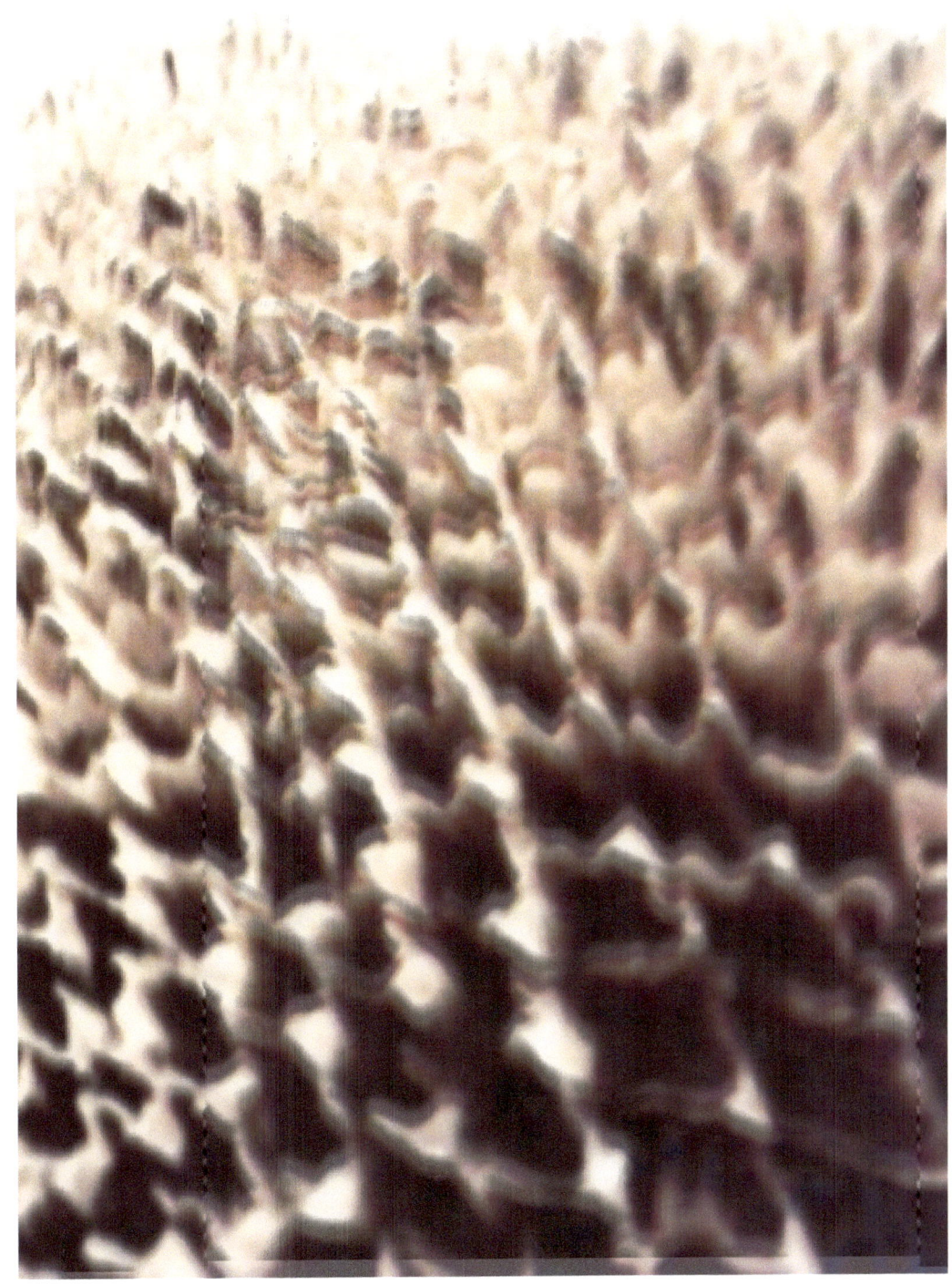

33 Interrogation is completely useless. It expects to transcend its context cleanly and to create an outcome that erases itself. Instead, the exorbitant energy it seeks to use as force is converted into an excruciatingly loud sound of error.

34 A weak force is one of radioactivity, of its decay. A force with no range. Weakness is no lack. It makes seemingly small adjustments, it shifts, it utilizes carrier particles, it winds its way without moving a muscle. ~~~~~~~~~~~~

35 Continually grasping at what has once been more solid.

36 Perhaps it is a mistake to think of language and words as whittling down or carving smaller and smaller distinctions. ~~~~~~~~~~~~~~~~
There are terms like 'continuous function' and others that help to evade distinctions between grass and ground.

37 In consideration of the question: where does the grass meet the ground? No 'where', no 'doing' no meeting', but maybe 'interference'? The interference of grass/ ground.

38 From Avital Ronell's essay "Worst Neighborhoods of the Real" from Finitude's Score, pg. 223:
Philosophical thought was never not starting trouble nor beyond contamination, and this may be taken in the strongest sense, perhaps in a way that is most abundantly underscored in Nietzsche's pathos of distance and his great politics of health.

39 When we follow along, we have the continual hum of reaction, division, and therefore of a togethering. The only thing we meet, however, is the linear history (however living) of chronological reactions.

40 From Aristotle's "Problems," Book XVII -Problems Connected with Animate Things, Number 2: Why do animals and plants grow more in length? Is it because increase in length is triple, in breadth double, and in depth single? For length is primary and from the beginning, such that (at first) it alone increases, and it again occurs at the same time as breadth, and thirdly at the same time as depth. But breadth is double, by itself and at the same time as depth.

41

42 If we hold on to the intended listener we become interrogators.

43 Interference in a meeting of two agents can be an activity of cancellation

instead of a sea of ambiguous pixelations. If both agents extend a greeting on the same wavelength, they may obliterate each other. Or they may reinforce each other. Enforcement or annihilation. The myths of the doppelganger usually entail annihilation.

44 We have to stop thinking of 'public' as being related to concrete. It is time to go to grandmother's house, even if she is a wolf.

45 Plants know how to reach far better than ~~we do~~ us. We could be more attuned to the elegance or inelegance of our grasp, our intent to grasp.

46 Does it matter if a plant is in a pretty pot or if cuttings exist on water, air and sunlight alone? Technologies of transfer don't seem to trip them up as long as they can meet their minimal requirements. Our shoddy notion of nature would have us believe that the complicated mess of forest is the only truth of nonhumanity, but there are complicated messes everywhere, with humanity ~~only~~ being one problem set.

47 The complicated mess is rendered unsuitable. We redact the alien, the alien becomes alien through redaction.

48 Transbstantiation as the conjecture of a felt concept with a visual sign

49 When describing how a weak force is able to change one quark into another, physicists often use the term 'flavor', that the weak force changes the 'flavor' of the quark. Taste resides, perhaps, deeper than touch.

50 Please touch the plant.

51 I invite you to indulge in your favorite food today.

52 Interpretation is mandatory.

53 Face-to-face. Tete-a-tete.

54 From Vilem Flusser's *Towards a Philosophy of Photography*, page #17:
The function of technical images is to liberate their receivers by magic from the necessity of thinking conceptually, at the same time replacing historical consciousness with a second-order magical consciousness and replacing the ability to think conceptually with a second-order imagination. This is what we mean when we say that technical images displace texts.

55 It is of utmost importance to understanding to create categories, if only to be stupefied by anomalies. The important thing, however, is to remain stupefied and not to interpret those feral things within us upon the screen of the anomaly's indifference.

56 Let us not forget about the meeting between two lovers. The inescapable edge of sensation and solitude.

57 What is captured by a lens necessarily includes the lens. Lens grinders have great responsibility.

58 Chance is the very breath of existence.

(5)

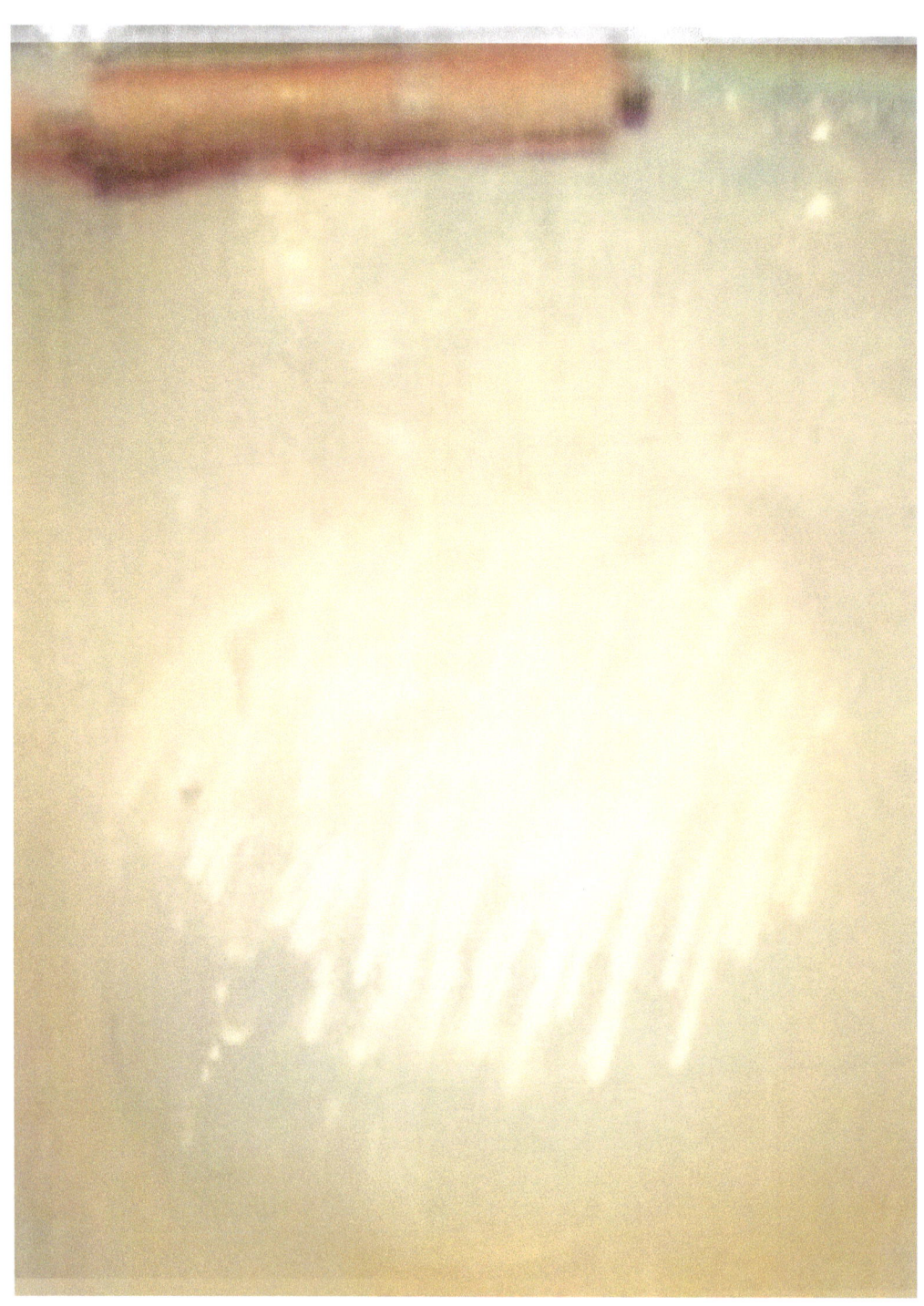

59 Whether arbitrary or intentional, the responsibility that follows choice is one that opens our determinations and allows for a new set of directive forces of our own choosing. Ultimately the apparition of choice helps to navigate the sea of chance.

60 I just witnessed a tiny mouse climb a tree. Some might consider this to be magical.

61 In general, the problem with esotericism/occultism/magic, is that in considering there to be sense outside of our empirical senses, it reinforces the misconception that we know all we need to know about those five senses. It is a shabby excuse.
   [or so]

62 Within the grassiest of grass and the deepness of ground we also use language as our medium to make humans capable of surpassing themselves while the plant is not seen as doing this. Is this how we substitute immortality for eternity?

63 From Simone Weil's *Gravity & Grace*, page 19:
   Time is an image of eternity, but it is also a substitute for eternity.

64 When we attempt to 'go back' or grasp the past as the only truth, we become feral children with bad manners. We must claim our childhood and our history, but we must reach out for our adulthood. We get to determine it and, in this sense engage child-like wonder. Remaining or reinstigating being a child, however, is merely a way of being taken along, but of our own forgotten sorrows.

65 Vital materiality has come to light via synthesis and following the rules stays within the playpen of thinking.

66
   * There are no human specific quarks. Nor atoms. Nor molecules. Our cells are created under human forming direction, directives. Our material only differs from our surroundings after processes that we are largely unconscious of.

67 We act as though there was only ever us as manifest content, but we forget about our latent content. Freud was on the right track in the way he saw us as manifesting machines, in the way that he gave creedence to the substance of the unconscious as our material for manifestation. The question remains, however, where 'unconscious' draws its lines. It has been argued that plants do not have consciousness, yet we are entirely reliant on plants and animals who eat plants to give us the nourishment we need to build our manifest bodies and thoughts and dreams. If you drink too much you become drunk. The manifestation of this comes (more than likely) from yeast.

68 Whether we like it or not, the world we consider 'nature' will balance itself. We are not equals. If we prove bad tenants, we won't merely be evicted - we will be subsumed and digested. The worm is king.

69 It is possible to feel a misunderstanding while it unfolds. We don't have to wait for hindsight. When options become limited and excesses prevail, it is because we misunderstand what actually is before us.

70   Ideology as a term to discuss the rigidity of communication has become rigid itself. Just as this statement has become a tautology. We want to be sure, so sure, so very sure.

71   ~~████████████████████████████████████~~
     movements

72   ~~████████████████████████████████████~~
     Caffiene, nicotine, aspirin... You, too, live off our poisons, namely carbon dioxide. But I wonder if we haven't made too many poisons, for you will soon overtake us. ███████

73   Sometimes there is nothing to say to a plant. Same goes for the unintended listener. My capacity ███████ seems to be decaying...

74   We make gardening manuals and diet manuals and cookbooks and materia medicas. In confrontation with this literature, this instruction, this information, it is possible to gain understanding if you are made of dirt.

75   It is a shame that people don't lose their chlorophyll when left in the dark, searching for the hintiest hint of light.

76   From Anne Carson's *Eros the Bittersweet*, pg. 55:

   The alphabet they used is a unique instrument. Its uniqueness unfolds directly from its power to mark the edges of sound. For, as we have seen, the Greek alphabet is a phonetic system uniquely concerned to represent a certain aspect of the act of speech, namely the starting and stopping of each sound. Consonants are the crucial factor. Consonants mark the edges of sound. The erotic relevance of this is clear, for we have seen that eros is vitally alert to the edges of things and makes them felt by lovers. As eros insists upon the edges of ███████ human beings and of the spaces between them, the written consonant imposes edge on the sounds of human speech and insists on the reality of that edge, although it has its origin in the reading and writing imagination.

77   We need distance. It is how we can feel the pull of our concepts.

78   As remarked earlier, ESP (extrasensory perception) is a sham. We haven't yet figured out, or come close to examining empirically, what ███████ ███████ our familiar ███████ senses are capable of sensing.
     To imagine plants as capable of ESP is to render them in our own mistaken identities.

79   Plants already tell us everything.

80   Flavors of quarks: up, down, strange, charm, bottom, top

81   Lovers often decay.

82   Let us not forget Raymond Williams and properties of culture:
              residual, dominant & emergent

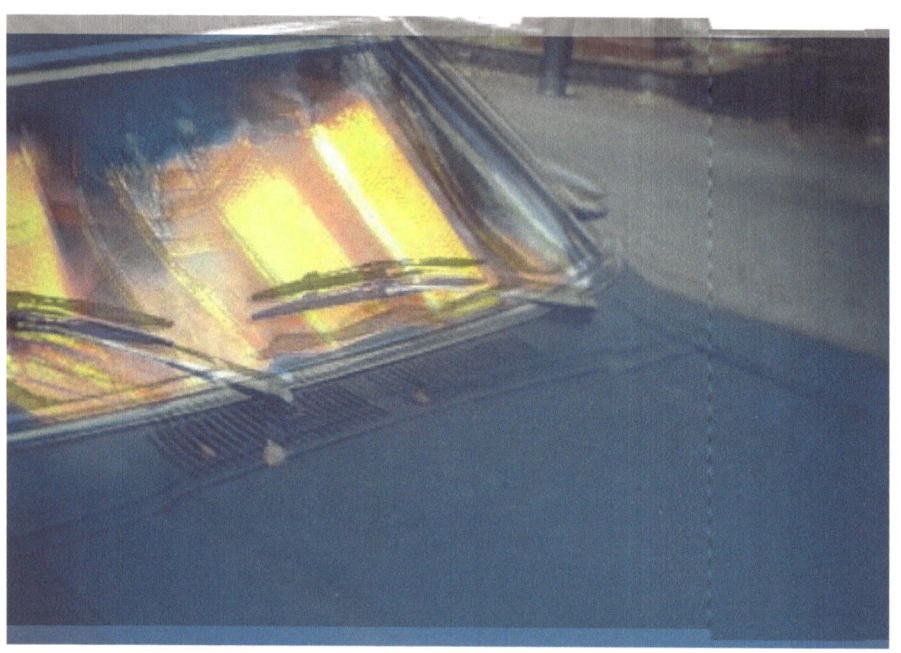

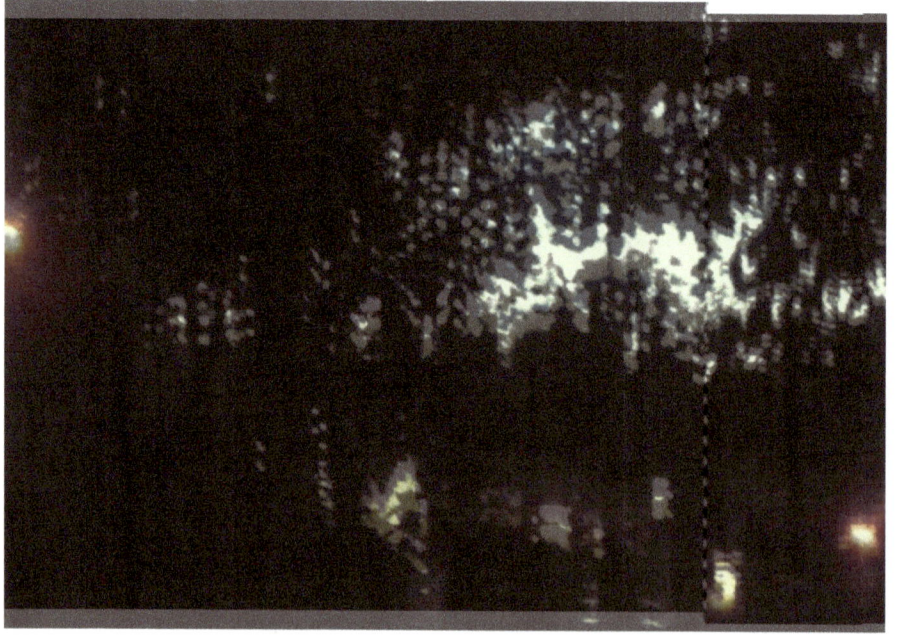

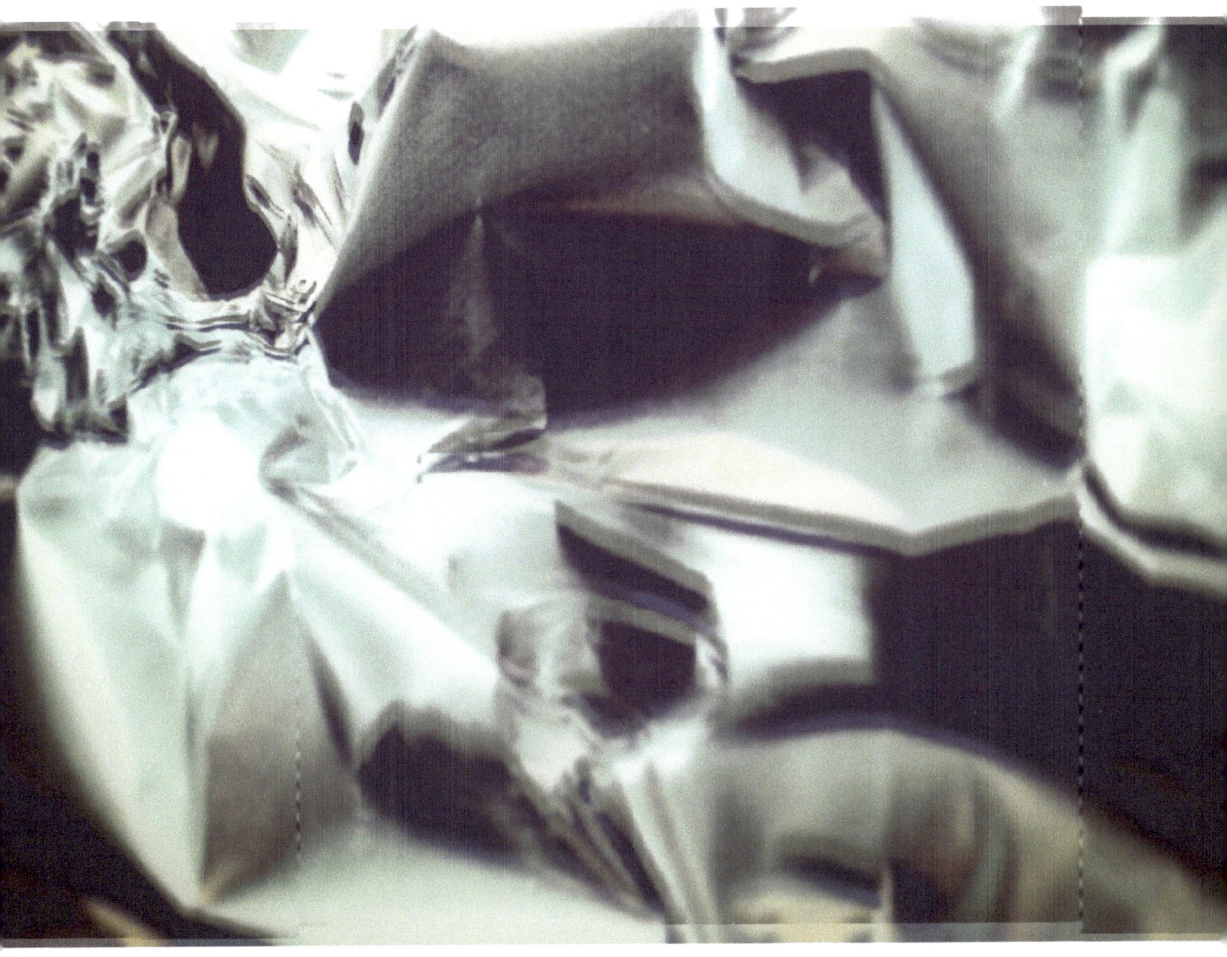

83 I listen to Nick Trotter and his music he made for you.

84 Continually grasping at what has once more been solid.

85 Could it be that our techne has its own being?

86 Understanding & interference, understanding interference. Where does knowledge meet understanding? We cannot 'know' interference, it is felt. Crying, weeping comes at points of frustration. Not sadness, not happiness, only at the, or in the, imponderability of feeling and the resulting frustration.

87 We have not even touched on the swamp. The marsh. Water, mud, champagne.

88 Yeah, the swamp is a neighborhood that alligators and crocodiles live. And bacteria and crawly things and amphibians. Although it is always a bit of delight to consider the salamander as a being out of fire.

89 To get to where the grass meets the ground, there is the possibility of starting a prarie fire. Perhaps this is the intention of rioting? But in our inability to clarify (as it should be) where or how, when the grass meets the ground, we muddy already swampy relations. We often miss the point. It is imperative to use small silent boats. Sometimes overarticulated technology cancels out perceptible signals in its attempt to capture our imaginations.

90 Three eternal principles according to Pherecydes of Syros: Chronos, Zas & Chthonie. Chronos: the personification of time. Zas (or Zeus): father of gods and men. Chthonie: as pertains to earth - in, under or beneath. Dwelling in the earth.

91 XXX~~████████████████~~ And so we are taken along.

92 Somebody will ~~████████~~ meet their lover for the second or third time.

93 Somebody will find themselves in an unfamiliar neighborhood.

94 Somebody will forget their briefcase.

95 Somebody will end up drinking a little too much wine.

96 Somebody will write to someone they've been meaning to get a hold of for a long time.

97 Somebody will, perhaps, dance.
98 Somebody will end up walking barefoot.
99 Somebody will sleep.

works cited

Adorno, Theodor W. *Problems of Moral Philosophy*. Trans. Rodney Livingstone.
    Ed. Thomas Schroder. Stanford: Standord University Press, 2001.

Aristotle. *Problems: Books 1-19*. Trans. & Ed. Robert Mayhew. Cambridge:
    Harvard Univedity Press, 2011.

Carson, Anne. *Eros the Bittersweet*. London: Dalkey Archive Press, 1998.

Flusser, Vilem. *Towards a Philosophy of Photography*. Trans. Anthony Matthews.
    London: Reaktion Books, 2000.

Knapke, Debra & Laura Peters. *Herb Gardening for the Midwest*. Auburn, WA:
    Lone Pine Publishing Inc., 2008.

Ronell, Avital. *Finitude's Score: Essays for the End of the Millennium*. Lincoln:
    Univer sity of Nebraska Press, 1994.

Weil, Simone. *Gravity and Grace*. Trans. Emma Crawford & Mario von der Ruhr.
    London: Routledge Classics, 2002.

Random order as determined by flipping through the first 99 pages of *Giving an Account of Oneself* by Judith Butler

1st 33
37, 24, 9, 52, 30, 88, 27, X, 41, 89, 48
72, 63, 49, 31, 15, X5, 99, 87, 65, 34, 19
79, 35, 13, 97, 54, 32, 22, 82, 17, 6, 91

2 nd 33
_), 60, 16, 4, 23, 95, 86, 62, 56, 21, 25, 78
28, 47, 66, 84, 8, X2, 44, 3, 42, 98, 89
64, 92, 28, 40, 70, 71, 10, M, 55, 75, 20

3rd 33
7, 96, 11, 94, 14, 93, 18, 90, X, 85, 26, 81, 29, 80, 33, 77, 36, 76 X
39, 74, 43, 73, 45, 69, 46, 68, 50, 67, 51, 61, 53, 59, 57, 58, 2

(9)

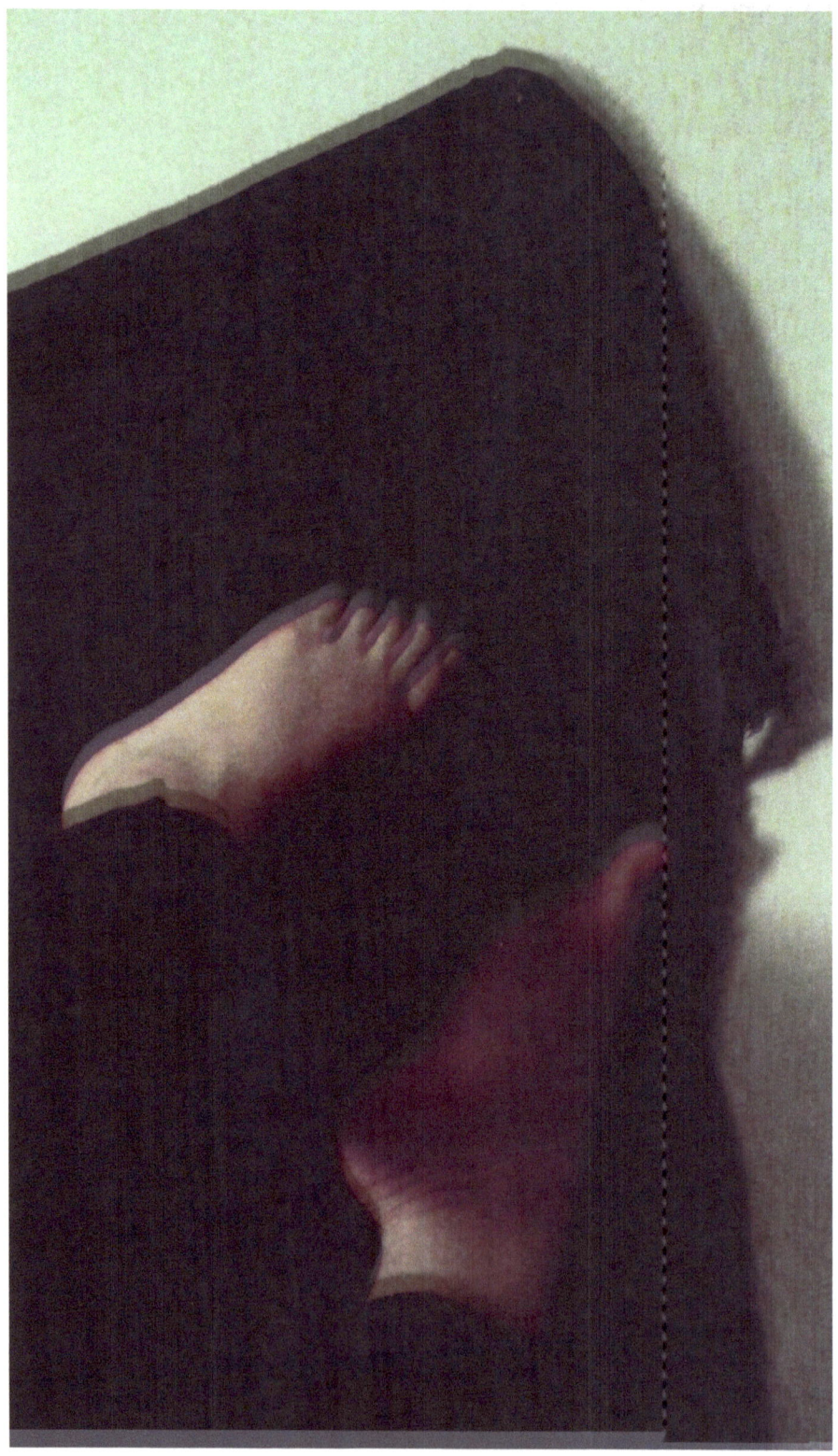

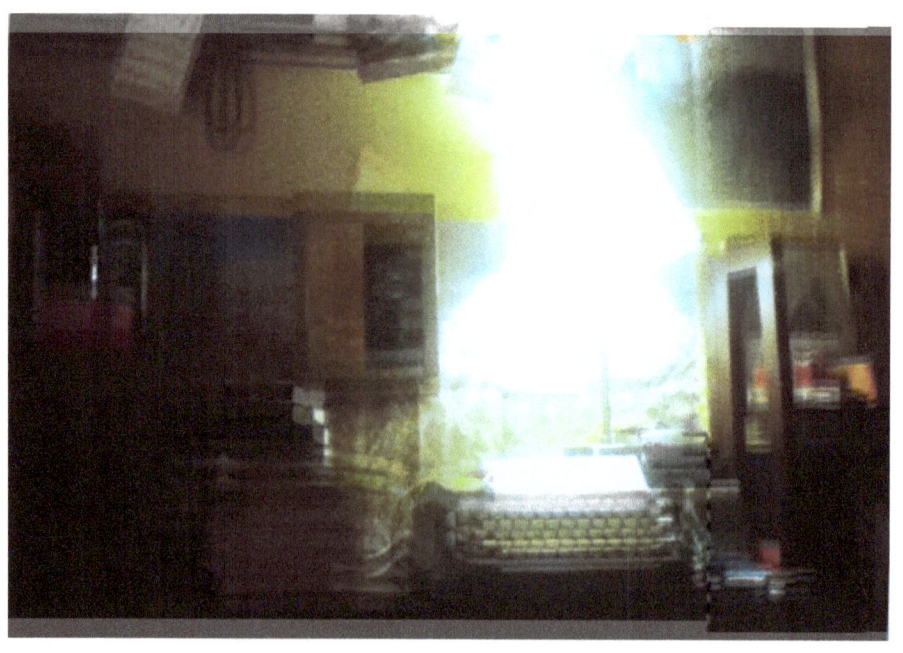

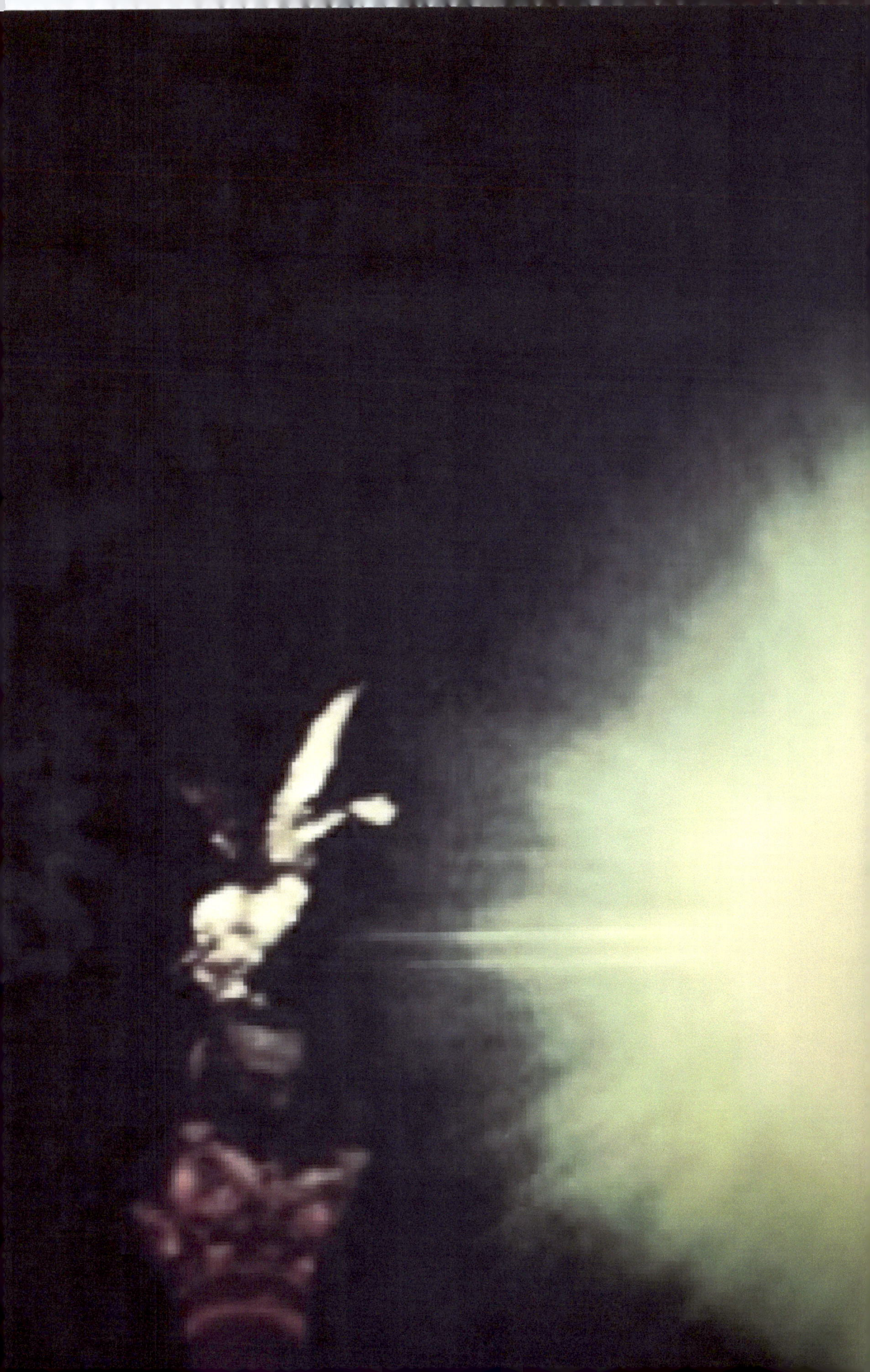

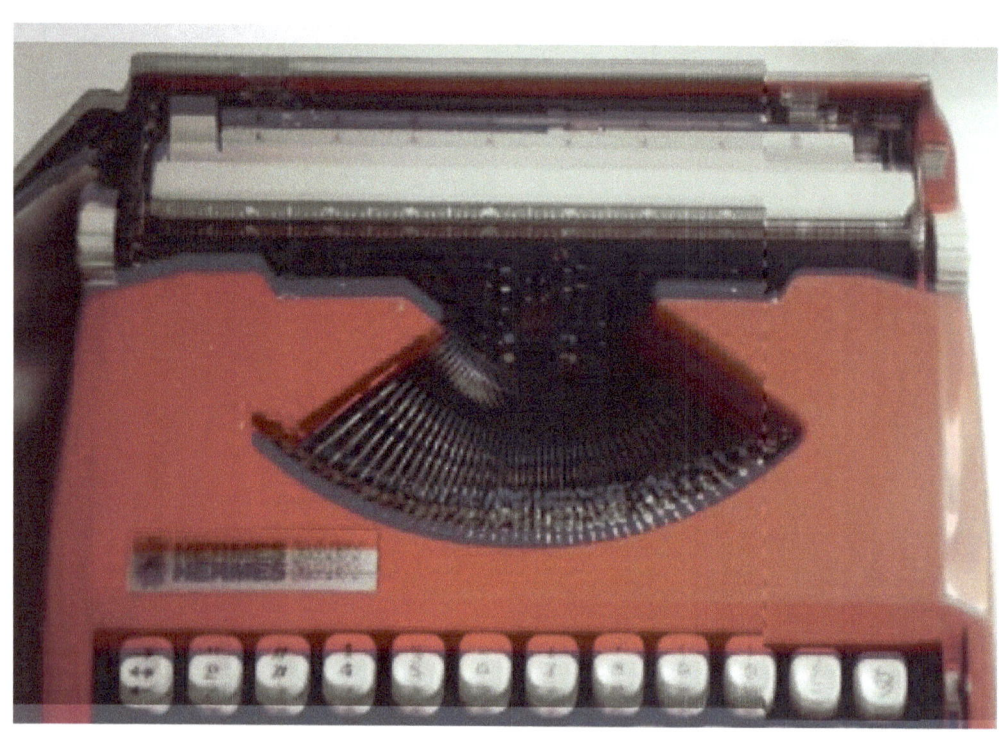

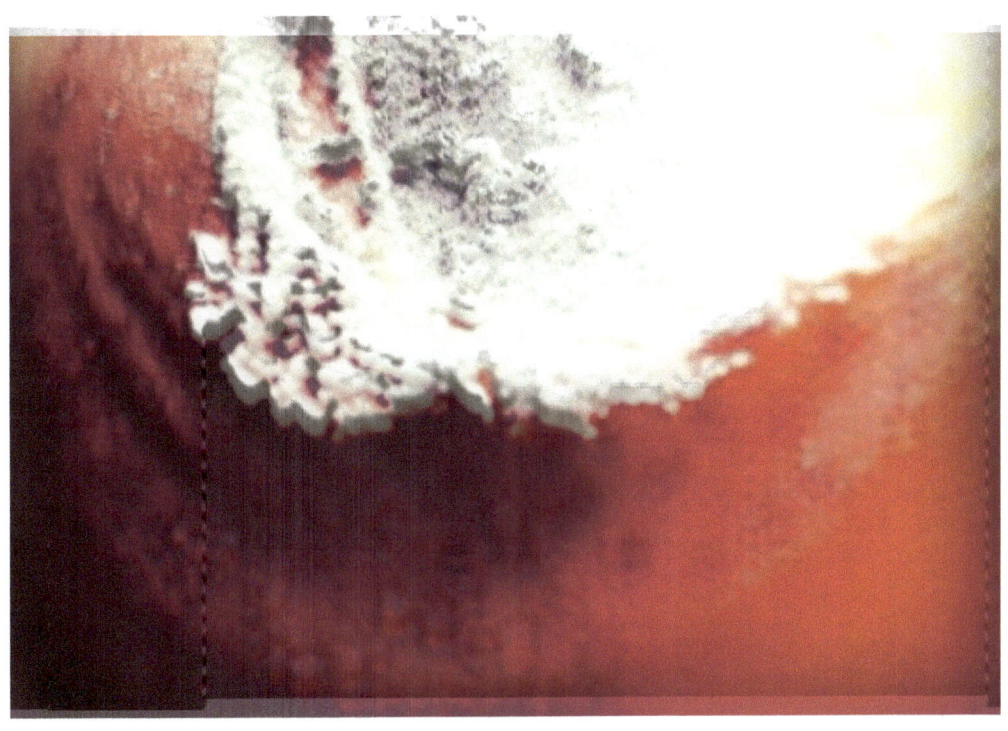

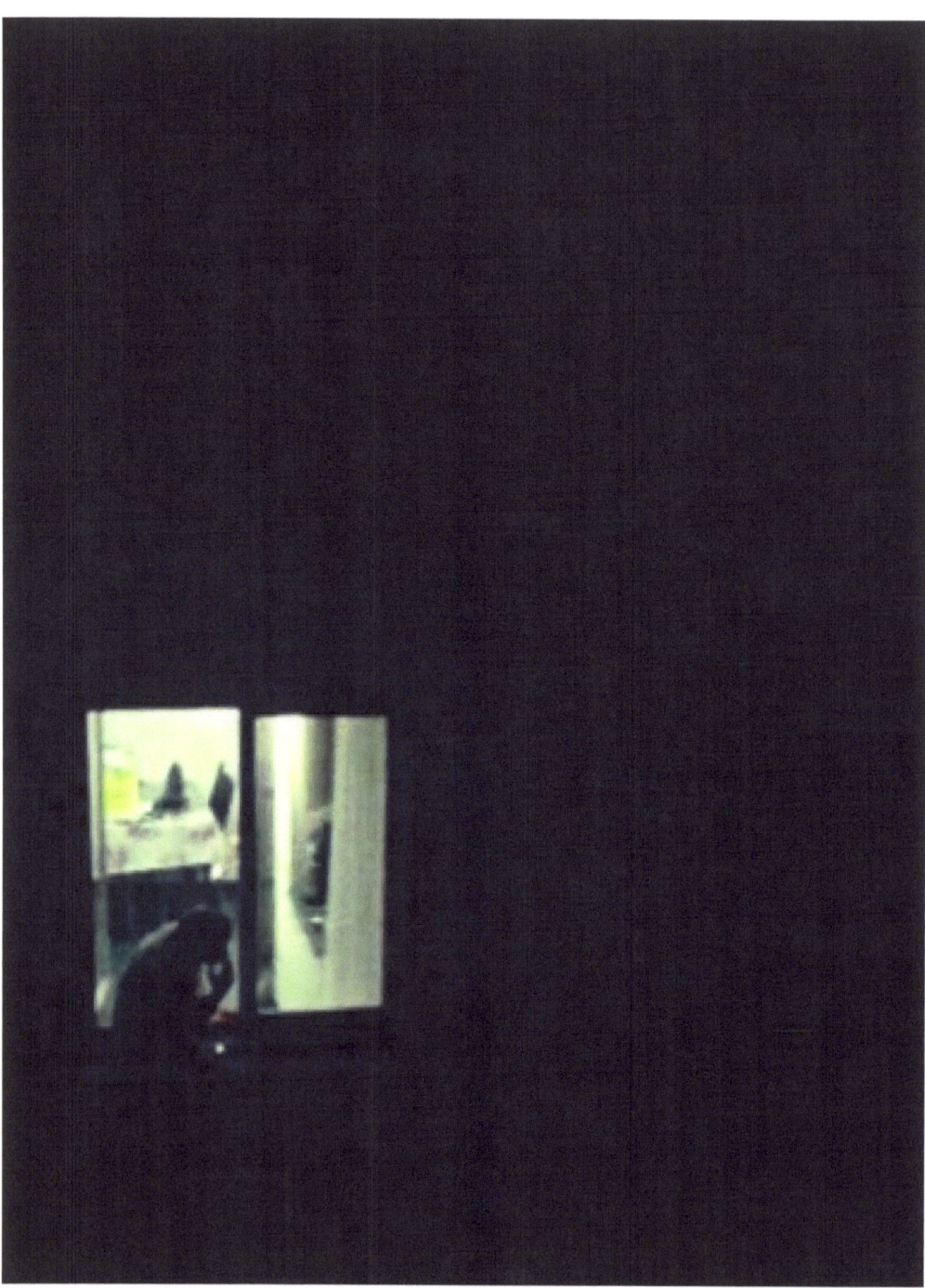

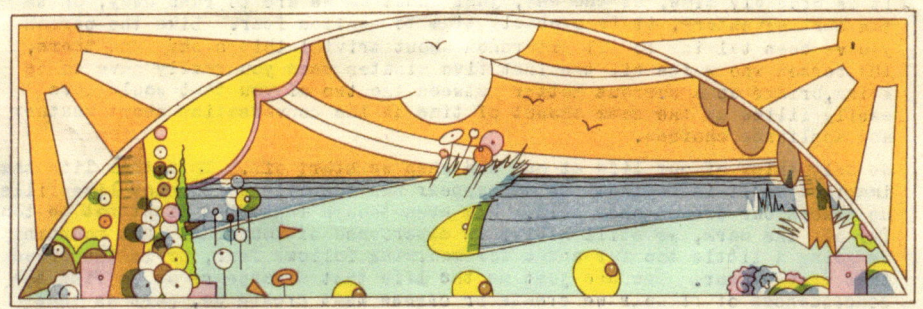

Let's imagine this.
walking down a street that when you remember later you will remember that time, walking down that street on that day, the day when the newness of the street passed into familiarity (but only memory sees this atmosphere of the day). Perhaps it is a year later when the memory is recalled, under the same falling leaves
And what is remembered is the anticipation of a new night spent with a new friend you already feel like you will remember in a certain light. But when you remember the day, the warmth of the pavement, the smell of an approaching cool twilight already present in the late morning air, a scratchy memory of rain in the gutters, , when the memory drifts back to you it lands on your skin that has already lived through the past that unrolled itself on the breath of that anticipation.

So you knew the anticipation was based yet on the unfamiliarity, and what became familiar
What became experienced and what remained in ever anticipation. And this environment of remembered anticipations. The certain lights that never consumed us in the way we thought we would remember them. And the way we held our hand, waiting to grasp that future memory, letting pieces of what will have happened fall to a ground, collect dust,and fill our spaces

Reacting to the past, it isn't the fruit we cling to, but the arch of the branch drifting to sleep under the weight of its results. Apple. Orange. We have relationships with objects not based on their qualities, those veils some scientists seek to lift –

not based on their qualities, but on their rhythms, the rhythms they produce to form the hand of our grasp. And what we think of as an object.

           s are less scary when they have a name.   nameless state

It is curious to think that we only communicate with what we think might answer us. As if understanding was ever reflected back to us. What can only ever answer us in our own words. Remember that Echo's infatuation was with a man who loved his own echo. XIx So even talking talking to a wall   reflection

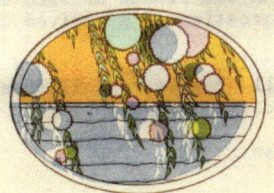

It is probably time, at the end, just about as we are to run away, on to your next adventure, to pay plenty of attention to things like the person who waits to tell the person about trivial things here and there; the person who waits for that lull between minutes when you really have to be going, brings up another matter between the two conversations that would have easily filled up the same amount of time as the conversation about weather and appliance choices.

We only think of our life at one end when we start off. Then we think of our life at one end when we start off. We think that life has no end and if we imagined a sufficient distance head, it might somehow live past the space we are in. And experience that life might not be too far off the mark. We still have this experience of mourning: But mourning that involves little to ensure a just, fearful ringing hollow after — or is the dread that addresses our futures, creates the life that disappears finds the consequences of failing we wear also ceases to be. What we fear is always that giving up of what once was.

If you are a person who thinks you are a person that doesn't like, say, olives, for example, and you meet a person who doesn't like olives, they don't exist to you. They have no impact. Until you accidentally or in some time lapse record, you are set in a person who let's say you ended up enjoying the experience. You are not a person who doesn't like olives anymore.

So sometimes, on matters more pressing, the fear of not being made up of holes in parts we once thought were solid, even of enemies, shock us. Make holes in what we once thought was solid.
What dies when we start to take on that the limitations we arbitrarily what dies when we start to take on that the limitations, we arbitrarily assign to who understands what and what understands who, that these limitations are but fairly tales.
are but fairly tales.

To learn anything we have to give away everything.
To learn anything we have to give away everything.
So what is sacrificed when we search for where the grass meets the ground?
So what is sacrificed when we search for where the grass meets the ground?

We want so desperately that words, pages, leaves, that containers for passing waves of leaves of these things are containers for. are present. are true. These only kinds of richness:
Autocorrect. Word processors. These tiny images, atomic sensemakers:
Leaves fall. Trees live. Wind blows. Trees bend.
Leaves fall. Trees live. Wind blows. Trees bend.
If there is anything like only future makings, sensemaking requires space:
If there is anything like only future makings, sensemaking requires space:
experiencing and then catalog ourselves for later surveys. We take argon for what? So entrenched onto what. What show of war ourselves for a job well done? An entry back into what we once thought was completed or to embark on new seas?
Continually we mourn
Continually we mourn

Given the chance to thoroughly embed our images upon a plant,
Given the chance to thoroughly embed our images upon a plant, we would mourn the death of that plant as much as a person. or plants we own as much as pets: as the things, vegetarians mind eating. Plants continually live outside of the makings. We mourn beside missions find delight. Confronted with this with pathos would bear the unbearable in finding ourselves may endeavor to tell us so much. We would be willing to ourselves so much as people and animals not so much. But it is the bifurcation of perceived duties that is the culprit:

Imagine the ritual of expressing gratitude before a meal, for
Imagine the ritual of expressing gratitude before a meal, for the things the server is dispatched to disrupt our capabilities for - this is not a trivial conversation with others besides ourselves.

If I should die before I wake
If I should die before I wake

What is the point to love only what we can see? Is it not what makes love scary, terrifying? Like falling when we stumble upon it?

There is a man, a boy almost running but still walking with a bouquet of flowers in his arms, of excitement, of wonder and framing our feeling of greatness, of excitement, of wonderful to be bringing flowers to someone you love. Perhaps this lover is only being painful, empty, or sad or misunderstood. Perhaps a flower wilted, a hopeful reminder of what was once living. Standing in a vase, neglected, they will wilt.

There is no point in talking to flowers. They only speak to us. Layers decay like knowing; awe produces blooms between our beyond the roses Believing, I mean knowing. Feet produce blooms, the sure of great doing back to speak and say each redactions of ourselves one we make out to reveal bouncing back from the glossy black redactions of the one of what opens itself up to us. we speak and speak, animated by the sight of what opens itself up to us. ✳

At this point you are fully aware that it is utter nonsense to believe talking to plants accomplishes anything, right? There should not be gained any imperative that to do so is good for your health or if you are tending to plants, or anything at all. plants — the hope of this writer, the tending to plants, humanity's issues to a plant — it is my express hope that you become a better lover.

Lovers always hold, are content, love amongst plants. grasped is one's own heart now. There is no ... lover expects of us, we ... it is always shape of their redacted, withheld unconfessed of us, we begin to see the shape of their redacted, withheld, unconfessed...

There is no doctrine of a good lover. Don't be lied to, don't let them When my flower merchant sells me flowers he always picks a good bundle. Some of the blooms are they ... new blossoming and baby blooms, is always the point of an afternoon when they make best of the and even bloom. the buds then not have biggest blooms sparkle, for becoming what the ends sees of the bud is needed. Take a chance to create before the becoming of the thing that is going. really then, at full set of plants of testing to do. Keep tempting the fading flowers. Even a houseplant encourages life beyond carry. Just strips away the of a home flower from your house plant is dying and beyond care, it is imperative to remove it from your living space.

Wherever will we be once we exit this tract of thoughts? Much has been surmised about the relationship between reading and travel. Where do you find yourself? What is a day's reading. What information feeding our consciousness, because that's how we imagine it, no? That we take in the world and somehow it turns into bits of knowable material. Whatever do we experience everyday that leads us to think to build the a notion of transcendence? I love the moments in time-lapse videos where something rather major happens to direct the flow drastically. The technology so desperately wants to reproduce its idea of a continuous flow, one dependable record of everything that constitued the way one thing became another. But invariably the time-lapse jerks, in small ways and more dramatic. It makes known the inconsistencies. I imagine everything we have before us in our day. How much is the small knowledge of the world that we gain by sight informed by what we see our hands doing? They are in front of us all the time, doing things. They are capable of doing so many things. And yet, I bet if there was a time-lapse recording of what only our hands did all day long for one day, and then another — I bet that many of the days would be the same. I bet we could see a familiar shape emerge. What would we look like? This embodiment? What if we weren't some projection outward onto the world, what if we took up no space at all? And instead of considering what we were made of existed on this side of the senses, what if our body, our presence showed all that came without? How many coffee mugs would we be made up of? What color dominates our day? Do we then appear as all the pages we pressed upon our faces?

We see words, we press them to our foreheads, but there is also the action of pressing them to our hearts. Or maybe we don't even complete the action of our own volition, we don't choose, or at least the feeling is not one of choice, that something will dig itself deep into our sensemaking space. Questions of heart and head, fancy bread.

Choices, choices, chance. When we make a choice we are responding to our memory of our self. a future, we could put it there, we could put it there because it is a question of space — not really time's, a future memory. We act as though we will have remembered. Remembered ourselves, remembered how we were and we were made as we are presently. Technically to be able to excercise that freedom of choice of will we so desperately for some reason cherish, we would have to amend our conception of who we will futurely be. Luckily that's up for us to decide, but rarely do we ever get distance enough from the surrounding things that press up against us that we can gain enough freedom

And we think that objects bend to our wishes.

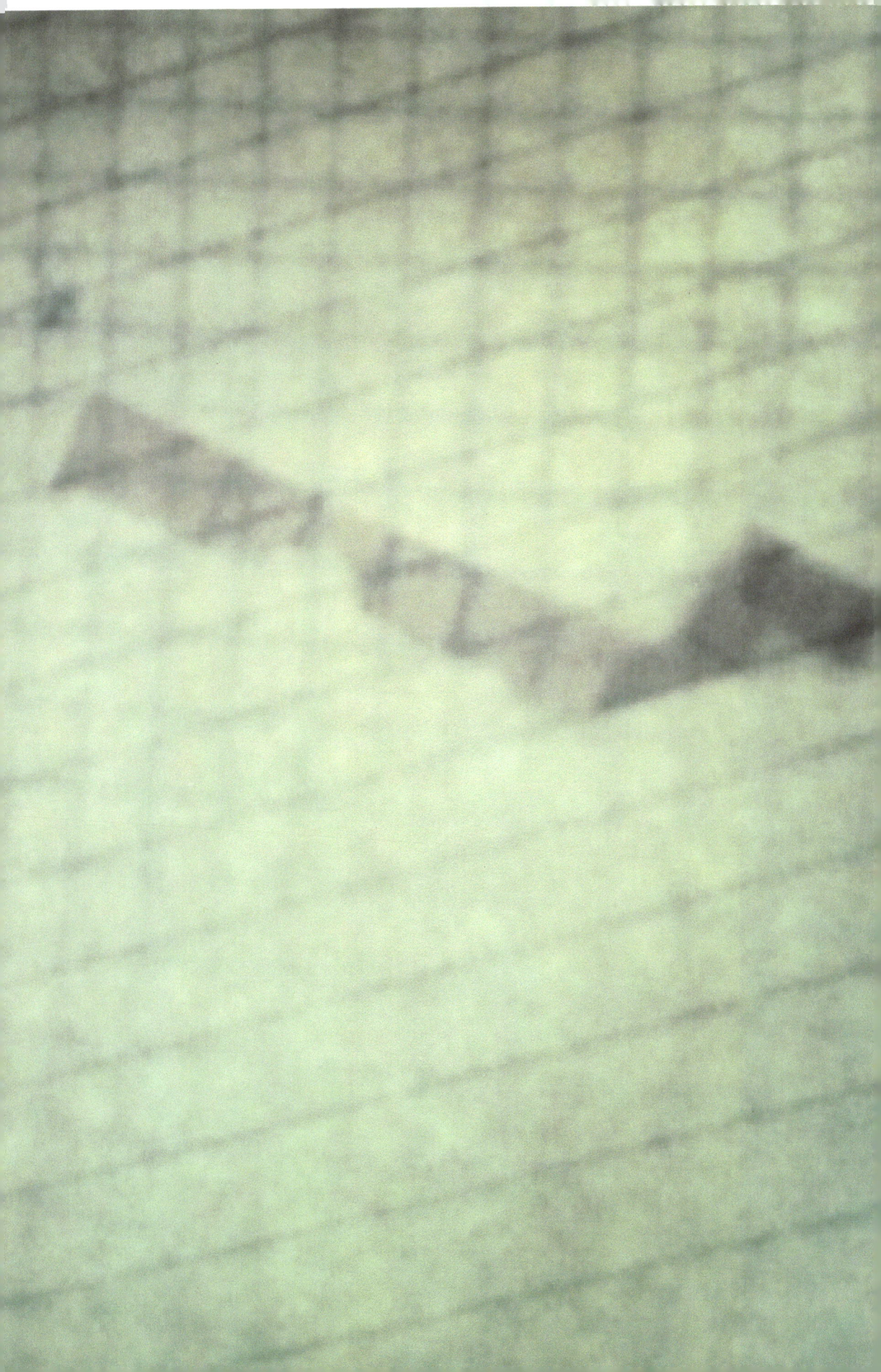

We've had a bit of an introduction. What do we know? The question, the problem with understanding of the aphorism, the problem with plants, with the loss of a quiet room where we can, in breath, breath, to hear the squeaking roof, the watering house plants into the turning soil, a small kissing noise, crackling is a spice like crack, of a plant that folds up at night is a priceless clock, especially when it is moody.

What we know now is beginning to appear the knowledge we are uncertain is an interpretation of the quiet we remain immersed upon the afternoon. Only the brightest when we can press through the dark cloth of night. When we can see other suns.

But for the moment, let's stick with our one sun and our millions of vegetables a bit, as direct and also to when direct others interest as we can want to be when we of course towards interpretation. These may to understand cooking understand interpretation perhaps to consider that understands it quite well. We perhaps consider that a tomato accomplishment though we remain deaf the tomato is speaking.

What makes a good cook is an ability to listen. Good plants require good cooks & plants. Good plants require good deaths.

Perhaps it is too soon for death. We can also consider gardeness good by successful tomato gardeners that growing basil near a tomato makes the basil that the basil deters the thrive in full sun but the basil sometimes the very same pests they may as well in that to feast upon tomato plants alongside basil in that the tomato tree on plant grown alongside basil in a tomato will take on some of the flavor of the basil rabbit; a touch is another vigoralist when tomato gardeners knows; there is nothing like pairing tomato & basil.

It is not our genius that made, that create deliciousness. genius that cook knows that they are not creators. humans and tomatoes are bridges between the world of humans and so many other worlds.
    Nearly every food is an aphrodisiac.
    Nearly every food is an aphrodisiac.

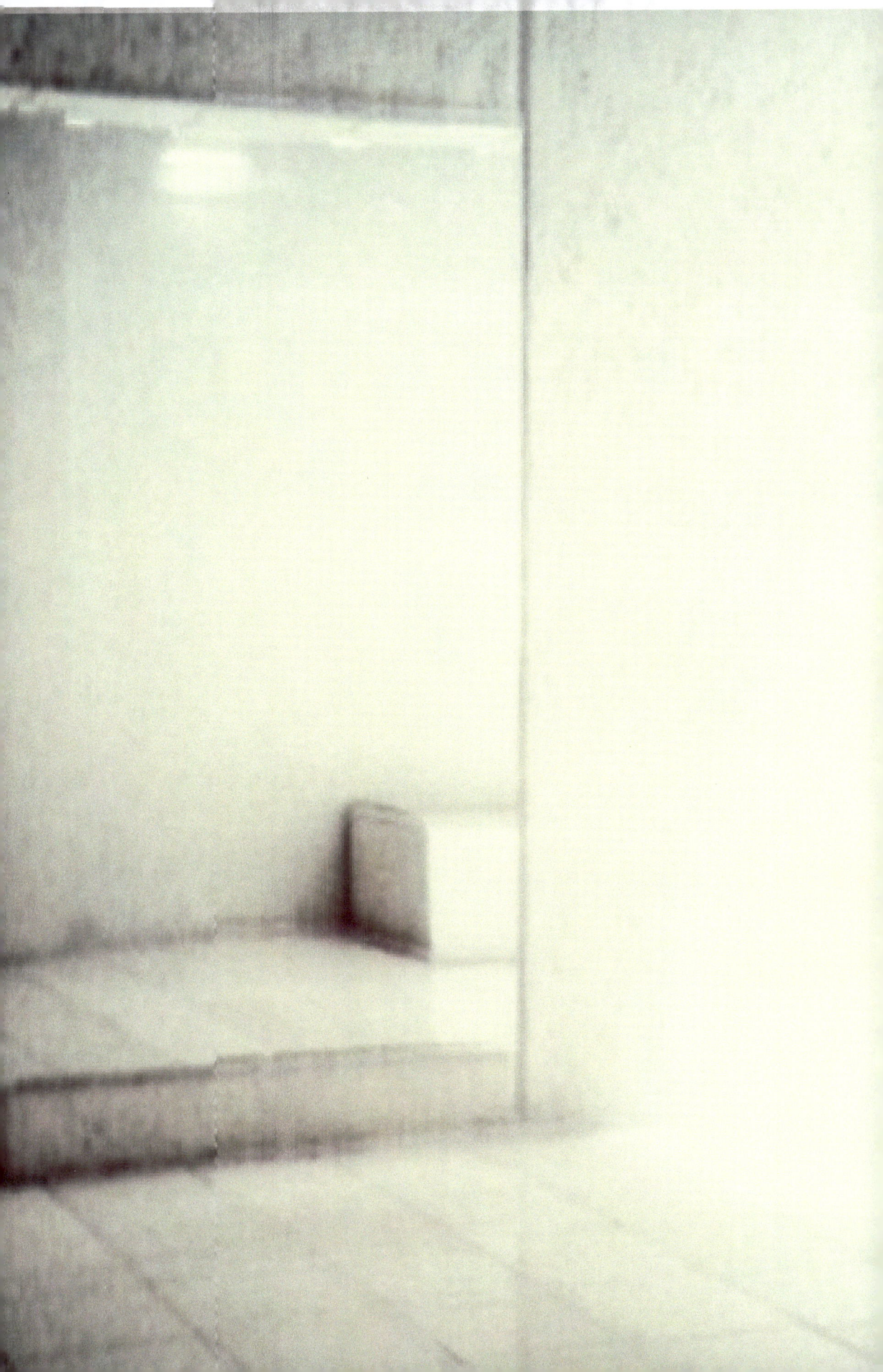

Have you ever attempted to use a tool you didn't
quite understand how to use only to marvel at someone
who was adept at its usage? Tools are not truth.
How we use them certainly will reveal many
possibilities, but as for the question of correctness,
there is only the exactitude of skill.

We can also mention recipes. The recipe is not, nor
does it contain the elements of what it instructs.
The ritual, however, has boundless history, is
predicated on history. Pictures, snapshots for
memory's sake. For memory's sake? If we ever found
where the grass meets the ground, would we remember
the location?

Evidence. Breadcrumbs. The tick of a clock. This
moment, that moment, this this this

There's no accounting for such things and , there we
are at the front of it all again. How to account for
one thing becoming another? Is it an issue of
complexity residing necessarily or one due to the
harness of perception? When do you know you will
leave a lover? Can it be possible to feel the
bitterness as it first arises? Or is it only when
we look back that we recognize that unnameable feeling
we had in our gut. We continue, continued a past
future. The difficulty of what actually cloaks us
indiscernable.

Don't get me wrong, it is crucial to have distance.
Critical.

The distance of time. Time which takes us each on
our own little way. Our own rhythms. Sometimes
others share our rhythm, lovers share the same time.
What is the importance of response time? The deeper
the cave, the longer the response time.

walls give us a safety of where we begin to be outside. We
depend on a certain tempo of echolocation. So to tell a plant a thing or
two is an excercise to either investigate a speed of return or to consider
that we may be looking long into the water when the space of our words is
addressing us. And through interference, we see walls where there exists
something responding by its very ability to remain, unknowable as it is.

16

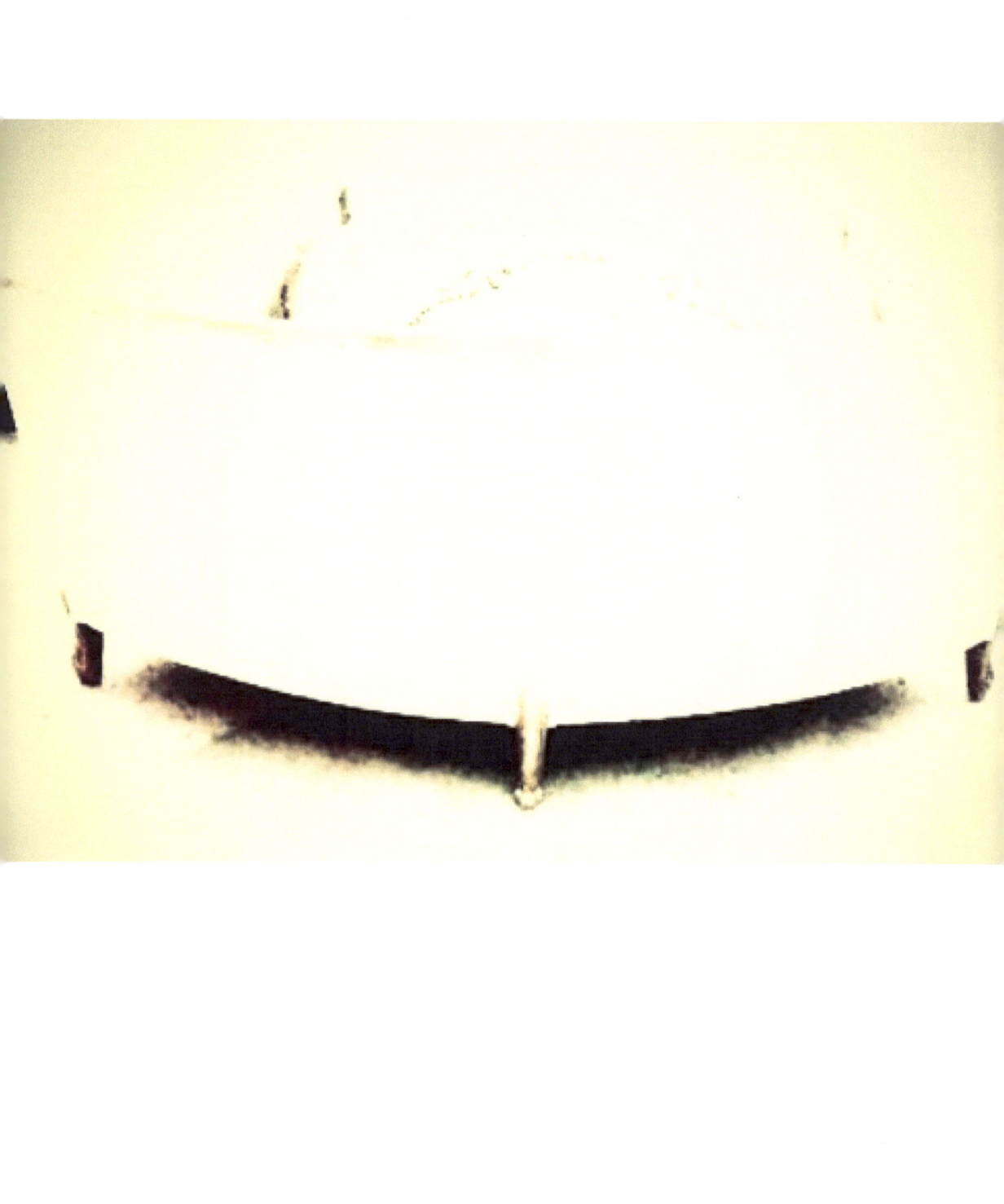

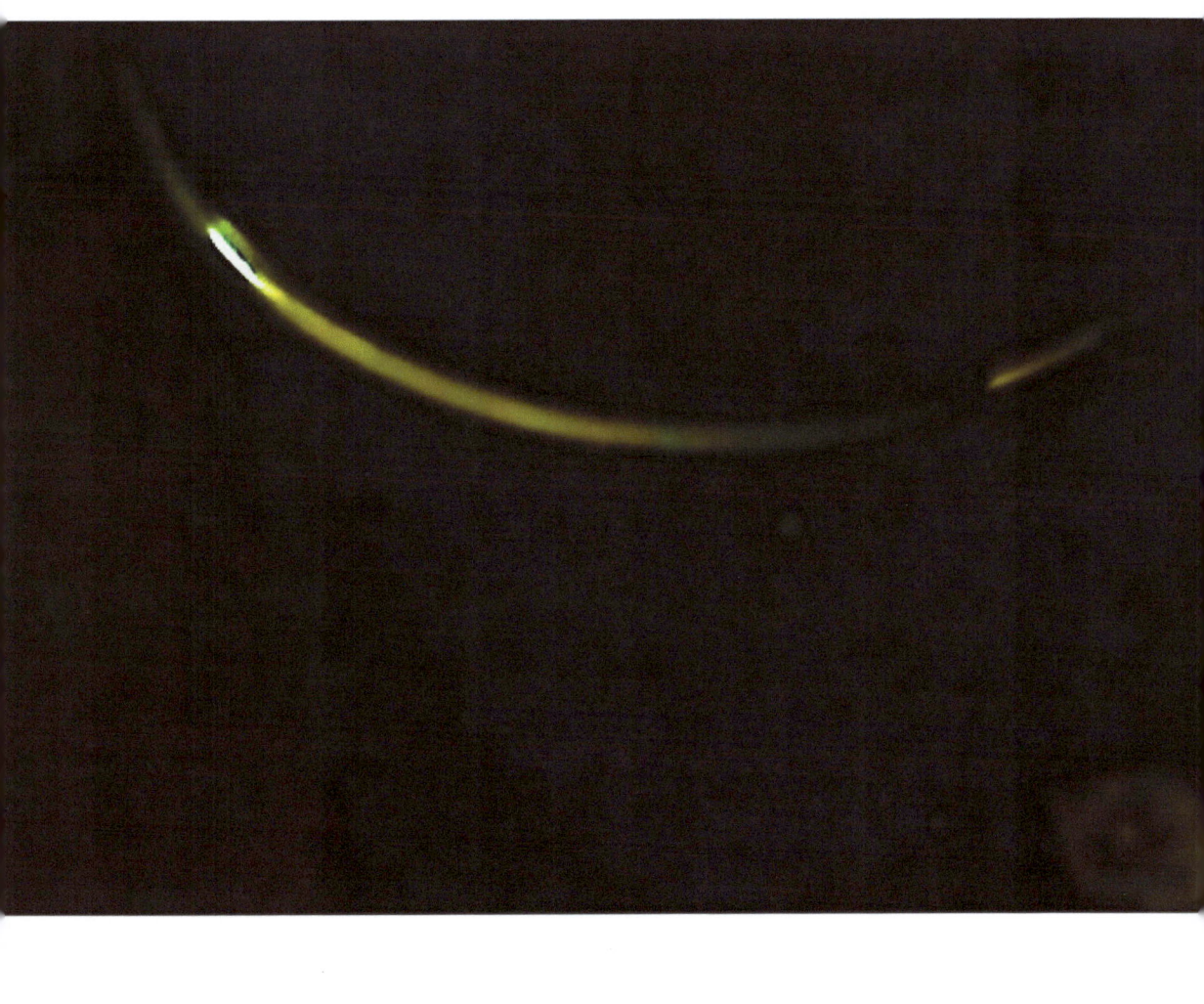

INDEX

. 1 . 14 . 40 . 41 . 15 . 42 . 43 .
initial step . how things grow or how we think things grow when we begin
to think about growing . fear of the result of unambiguity . eavesdropping

. 2 . 16 . 44 . 45 . 18 . 48 . 49 .
reacting . of course, and responding . the messiness of actually putting
forth every single word . inference . inferred there under though concrete
is a complex glue of how one thing becomes another under the veil of
ritual : the veil of using words descriptively for movements we don't
yet know

. 3 . 17 . 46 . 47 . 19 . 50 . 51 .
framing . &messes . we really can't help it . thank heavens

. 4 . 20 . 52 . 53 . 21 . 54 . 55 .
science and its limitations . seeing through the lens of science . en-
lightenment thinking . during the days we think we see everything but
above us is the blue shield keeping us from seeing outside ourself

. 5 . 22 . 56 . 57 . 23 . 58 . 59 .
meetings . scheduled meetings . chance meetings . choosing what represent
a meeting . reposibility in reproduction . what grows from what ground
we fertilize

. 6 . 24 . 60 . 61 . 25 . 62 . 63 .
magic . eternity . perhaps the most difficult movement . contagion and,
techne's relationship to being . goddam magic . accounting for beyond
but I already said that

. 7 . 26 . 64 . 65 . 27 . 66 . 67 .
seeds . our fertilizations . the kind of materialism that has
become popular because we have at eye level . or understood our way . seed-
the philosophical issue of our rites . according to Luce Irigaray we don't
forget; at one point the question of what women want was also posed by
those who wanted to understand more about the world, and
how we ask the same . objects already this claim that we do not speak as we
expect them to respond . are . as Irigaray's claim . a sexual difference . how
our feminines . masculine . about each . one my father always told me "
"feminism" frees men as much as women

. 8 . 28 . 68 . 69 . 29 . 70 . 71 . .
human hubris . 9 . 30 . 72 . 73 . 31 . 74 . 75 .
(we've been working on this eye already, like some others, but pg 1-3
cover this nicely)
. 10 . 32 . 76 . 77 . 33 . 78 . 79 .
interrogation . confession . one bit more magic . listening to the hard
bits when it is the soft ones talking

We really have yet to have a proper conversation, you and I. But what to say about us? I will have been long gone when you are ever yet to arrive. Still, you are already present as I remain. The ability of this shape, not unlike fire

and by fire I mean the swamp these words will get sucked into. Breakfasts, walks, tables, rugs, pets, plants, the lighting, the way you will remember the lighting which won't be the same as the lighting that still lights the same room. I mean the lighting that will have remained with you from the morning when you woke, the rooms you passed through, the weather - then you were in this lighting. Lighting which very well may change from one end of a sentence to another. My lighting has changed since I began writing these pages. And yet there is much to cover. And already we have arrived at fire.

I always hated reading books when the author addresses the reader as if it was absolutely certain in the mind of the author who would be reading their words. Sometimes the text doesn't even have to explicably state an address to be addressed to a subject. I do, however, have a certain taste for writers that anticipate a kinship, although the   that comes across in these sentences often can't help but reproduce melancholy.

You can tell quite a bit about an author in their whispered address, like planting instructions. The light they reach toward. Why not reach toward plants, plant-like plants?

The time we take to do these things. What other things can/could we be doing? The time we take, the time we spend, that passes, that we kill, waste, profit from, procrastinate. We are sometimes led to believe that all we have is time and it isn't entirely false. Perhaps it is only time that interferes between grass and ground. Time-lapse videos of plants growing entice us the way a flame tells a history in a flash.

A flash captures movement, they say, freezes it. Like the sharp edge of consonants trapping vowel sound in an echo. Capture is an important tool of understanding what exists around us, through us. We can investigate. Crime scene photos. Holding a truth just beyond our fingertips. If we were there, if only we were there. Postcards. Keepsakes. What do we actually remember when we look at a photo of our younger selves? What do we expect to know when we look at the photo of another?

We consider plants to be still, inanimate sort of, we can't hear them unless we get real near and then only if we go near on a regular basis. Their sentences are long to understand. If recorded, plants show incredible movement, indiscernable.

When do we start remembering our lover?

It can be tremendous fun to be in love. Probably for good reason.

Nietzsche, Postkarte an „Unbekannt"
(nicht abgeschickt); mit der Maschine
geschrieben am 16. Februar 1882

NEIN ES WIRD SO LEICHT KEIN GRUND
UNSRE SEELEN TRENNEN
UNMÖGLICHER ALS JEDER GRUND

What makes certain neighborhoods dangerous is not that the components that make up said neighborhood are in themselves dangerous, and certainly not that we will become infected by whatever we imagine transpires in said neighborhood, because, I mean, come on, no. A neighborhood is made up of the same things of no matter where it is: families, homes, patterns of survival-patterns of coffee drinking, young joyful people having young people awakenings, old people holding knowledge of past and future, patterns of walking, going to work and coming home, patterns of a so-called talking. No: when we come to the idea of a sensed dangerous neighborhood, we are correct in sensing danger, of course, but we misplace where the danger stems from.

We travellers, we movers through life, communicators, those not at rest, we are volunteers, voluntarily searching. This is the danger, no? Inescapable, lest you begin to think to stay shuttered away from the world knowing you hold your own disease. Even the most cloistered of communities cannot survive on their own productions. Consider the issues of inbreeding. Consider mad cow: disease, a disease that also occurs in cannabals if they eat the flesh of relatives.

Even dead, we move. Decay.

Again, like the consideration that speaking, or the plastic concept of speaking, is merely one of our limited ways of calling out something quite a bit bigger that happens, that we participate in simply due to our presence. Life, death, both demarcations in time of a very same thing. We try so very hard to make sense of things that are monstorously larger than things within the limited lens of time. We are hooked. Time and light. Trains and cinema. All our tricks are up one or the other sleeve.

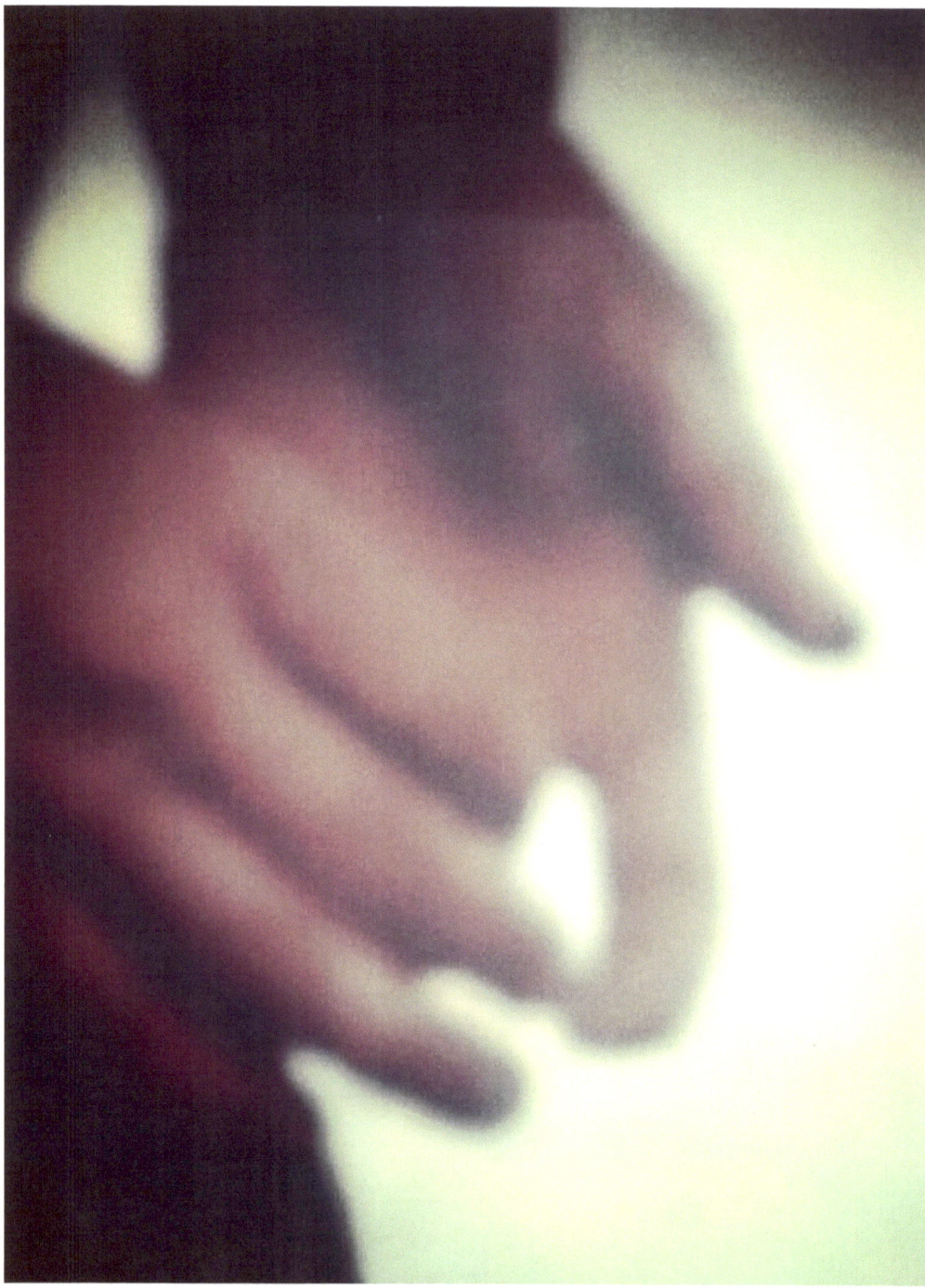

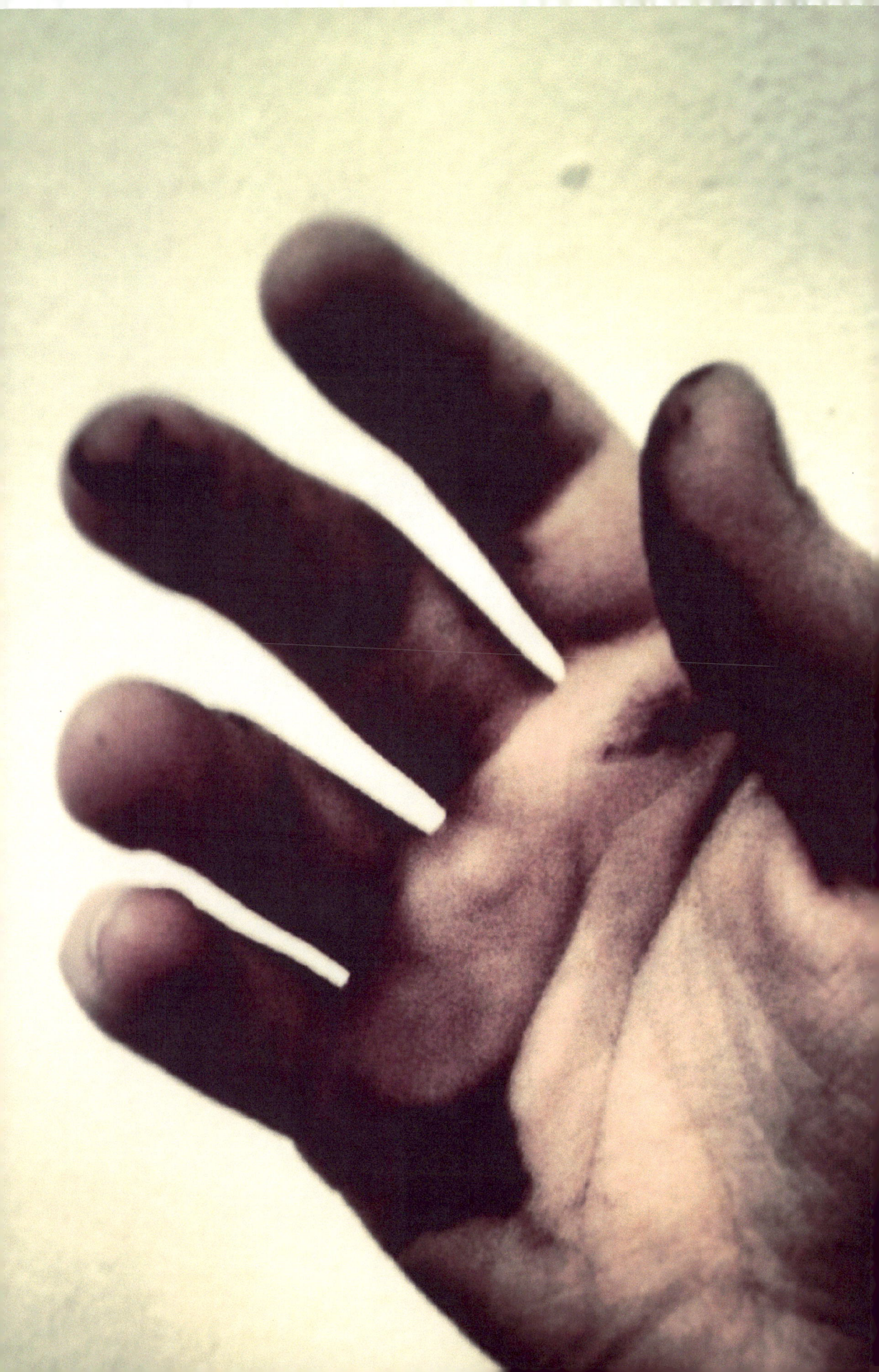

We are running out of things to
say, as is usual. At some point we
must leave this realm of consideration.

We will go back to our lives, make our
coffee, our tea. Eat food, watch films.
Talk to people, walk down streets, pass
by plants that are manicured, growing as
weeds in sidewalk cracks, sitting in pots in the
sun, harvested and sold in grocery cases. We may
remember the time we read these words or not. We
will experience problems in our lives and work to
find solutions. We will be happy sometimes and then
unhappy. We will forget our ages, and then, we will
remember to weed our gnarly parts. We will read, we
will fight for our own small injustices, we will
have dinner, go dancing, stay at home. We will
encounter danger and the like. Meet lovely people,
meet annoying people, meet people who initially are
lovely and then do great damage to our hearts, meet
idiots that surprise us with their capacities.

We will always be failing and succeeding at something.

We have our rituals, and we will fall into them
over and over. How we become ourselves everyday,
moving through our mazes. A ritual is never new,
we are rarely new. If we were licked by a flame
it would not consume us immediately. It would
bend around our curves, already present,
deepen the warps on our body, already present,
already sympathetic. Free will? Toss a log
into a stream and watch how the stream bed
changes over time.

If we commit the same ritual with different
words or clothing or whathaveyou, it still
yields the same results. Emperor's new
clothing and all.

There are words that do things, but my
best guess that it only looks like that,
a glaring symptom that appears it needs
to be treated when a larger disease
is at play.

The time we take to make them, the
time we take to think them.

11

Sometimes we think we are accepting new thoughts into our constellation of sensemaking. Breakthroughs. Advances.

And sometimes we freeze.

And sometimes the new thoughts we think we are having end up too fragile to keep. Consider the self-help book, or those programs we put ourselves through in the name of self-improvement. Desires to "change", to "grow": Diets. Education. We may feel entirely new to following a practice we have yet to be accustomed to, but to truly change, grow, what have you, can only come from the ground already growing us. You simply won't get a pineapple tree to grow outside in Alaska. That's why real metamorphosis is so terrifying, groundless until more fertile soil is found.

The science eyeball can only detect what emerges, and it does a fine and necessary job of determining the qualities of the thing emerged, revealed as well as (sometimes) the ground from which it emerged—but only from the expression of these properties within the already fled emergence. Consider considering if plants have understanding. Two methods: 1) to go by what we have come to understand as understanding on our own playing field, for example, plants do not have a recognizably similar nervous system in regards to our own. They don't scream like we scream like some animals scream. 2) to follow the hunch that perhaps we can understand more about understanding by guessing at how a plant understands.

The scales are so far tipped in favor of 1 that any movement towards 2 seems to be a wild assertion, hoodoo, an elimination of everything we have built thus far. But really, it is neither both. If we practice listening to plants, we will only discover dimensions yet unexplored of our own understanding. When we love it is our own hearts we grasp.

XX Considering objects: plants remain untolerably foreign, a life of their own before and after us indifferent. Unspeaking objects, darlings of materialisms, these are the tails, trails of human subjectivity. Once this is understood, then consider

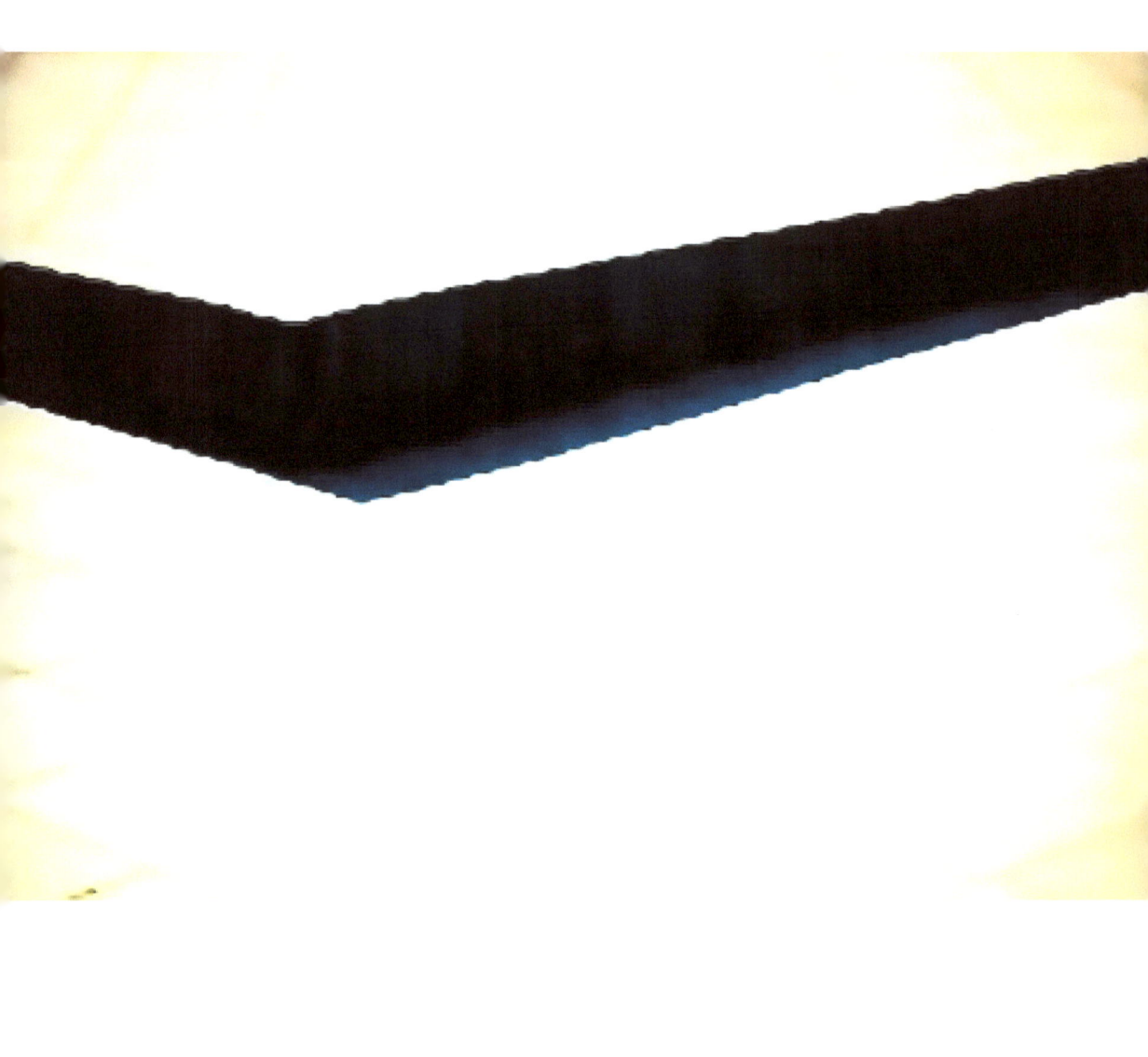

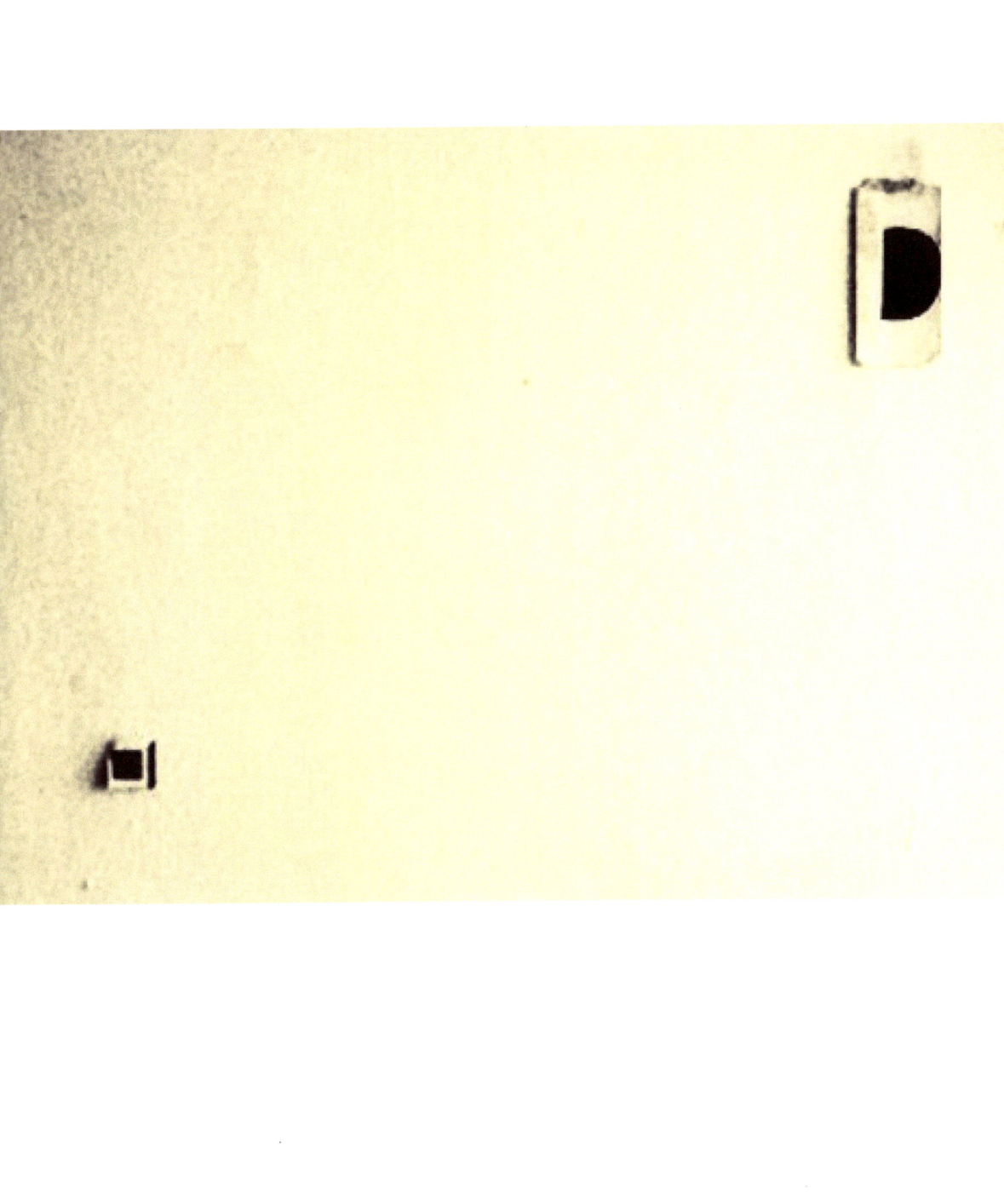

We are not that far away from talking to rocks. Not really that far at all. Something older, perhaps. There are those who believe in the healing quality of certain crystals, and certain healings based on the taxonomy of crystal as well. To believe in something, to believe that something can affect you, whether you understand each step of its workings or not; well, this is not out of a frame of science that allows for the power of a receptive framework. If you seek, you will find: problems & answers

Same for finding love. As if it is something to be discovered.

When we realize love cannot be found, discovered like a new continent, a new land. When we realize it is all we ever had access to, anyway, that old thing. It is not hard to see the old debate whether philosophy comes from disappointment and/or wonder.
Plants reach out for the light (in varying degrees), but they seek light. Those living find it all the time, but yet they continue to grow towards it. Regardless.

Watching a fire for long enough. The flames form amongst the pieces of wood, sticks, paper. No wonder the soul is often considered fire. It is molded, entrapped, guided by the physicality of the wood or charcoal. But as its burn wears down its limitations, the flames begin to shape the wood in its own curvature, its own escape routes, egress paths. Also there is driftwood. Less intense; more wet = less ash.

Metabolism.

Also see: turbulence
sand dunes

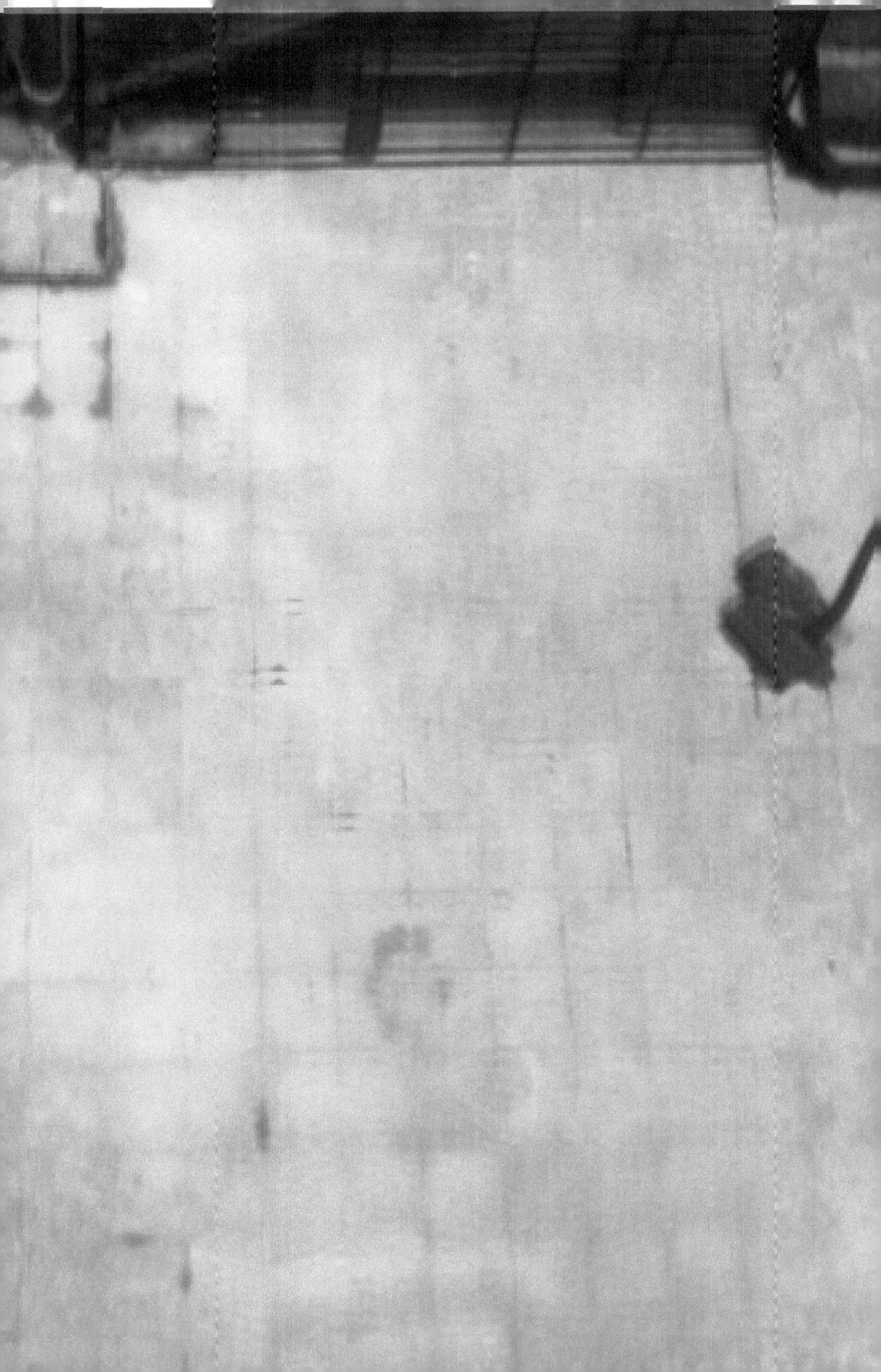

MORE INDEX

. 11 . 34 . 80 . 81 . 35 . 82 . 83 .
we try so hard, we don't do well in our
ever growing relationships with people .
finding guidance . decaying & what remains

. 12 . 36 . 85 . 86 . 37 . 87 . 88 .
attempting to explain and failing . the
fecundity of swamps . Solaris (either
written by Stansilaw Lem or filmed by
Andréi Tarkovsky) would be helpful here,
the conversation, the dear little speech
by Snaut, after they lose gravity
    (or Snow)

    Why do you think alien planets are .
       often represented as swamps, anyway?

. 13 . 38 . 89 . 90 . 39 . 91 & 92 & 93 &
           94 & 95 & 96 & 97 & 98 & 99 &

hope . home . what actually happens even
though we ¡think! we have entered the realm
of understanding for a moment, as if we
have scheduled that we will encounter
understanding between 7 & 9 in the evening
at an art gallery or reading a book or in
a class, as if we will fold it tidy like
our laundry, file it in a dossier to be
opened when it is needed, as if we would be
able to discern that future time when it
sweeps over us. Yeah, right. We are
reminded to take another look at what
we consider contamination. We are also
reminded of alleyways (but maybe that's
just me). When we consider, or when I'm
told something is dangerous, I always want
to know the specifics. Robbery? Violence?
What kind of violence? Often, I think, it
is the danger of becoming contaminated. &
& I use first person here, specifically,
    because I urge no one to become contaminated
by this inability to recognize danger...

7

Looking at our language -- and damn we are
already in the trap with 'looking', seeing as
believing, using the words of our oppressors.
But begging, "beginning" the question at this
intersection. We are a looking people when=
once we become literate. Before writing we
could assume it to be more natural to say
"hearing our language" when we wanted to explore
its nooks and crannies. lol stuff, really, but
we are exploring this at ground level, where
the grass meets the ground.
      We have come to thinking of words, the
fodder for knowledge, the measure of knowing,
explaining, we think of words and then of some
kind of language as the epitome of our human
face. And it is our surface, our edge, an
ability to form, give form. And sometimes we
use the language of language, of words and
seeing words and yes still hearing words, and
sometimes still words on a page, we say they
speak, speak to us. And sometimes we say
such things that are not words speak to us, it
is an easy list: colors, landscapes, moods...
whole sets of things without voices. My
suggestion is that instead of considering a
usage of speaking, as related to a kind of
anthropomorphic centrism, that we instead see==
(dammit, that see, that sticky perception)==
we come to interpret this way of relating our
own way of engagement, speaking-as=something=
having-to-do-with-words-and-or-language, as one
expression of something we as yet do not
understand, have language for, what we cannot
yet see.
      It is just a suggestion, but these words grew
from its ground. Plants have edges, too. And
we meet those edges with our own. It takes
more than a camera to investigate where these
edges meet. It is we who remain in the dark
without consciousness. Left to interpret what
we can with our limited resources. But we try
                we try ever
                we try ever so hard.

s meant to be eaten, it is created for another thing. The fruit is meant to be eaten, the seed is meant to be deposited with the fertilization of another. Chance is the operation here.

What does hygiene accomplish if not the blind hubris of modernity, our fragile lives that say should not be tidy. Only that so often this does not impart that we should not be tidy, fertilizer be damned, a houseplant wonders why our houseplants die. We live on the side - Plants and still we wonder why our houseplants die. Plants have a hard time living like us, well, like so-called modern, developed people. Of course there are those who are exceptional at getting houseplants to thrive. It takes a good care, an exceptional attention, a house raised on the health of a potted plant understands that care. In attempting to formalize the conditions, but our lives are never as clean as all that.

a dried up plant signifies the inability of its caretaker to in general, a dried up plant signifies the inability of its caretaker to remain aware of rhythms of life outside their own. Too much water, too frantic - only able to see need as one thing.

There is hygiene and then there is taking care. It is beyond hearsay, but koan, or perhaps maxim, of a cryptic sort for hygiene - that the luckiest person is the person with a clean toilet. That to maintain the cleanliness aspect of your bathroom, you have the time to followed that you have time to keep sacred of daily life, then toilets, water, drains, pipes. Curiosity cabinets.

Plants, toilets, water, drains, pipes. Curiosity cabinets.

ly a new thought that our environment reflects our interior although customs are the products of conscious escape this claim: it's rather a phenomenon of self-help psychotherapists, shuck organizers. interpreters we fresh phenomenon psychotherapists in reference to writers. But really, we remain steered vexed because we still own black and white thought what escape naturally offered a reduction. But still, it's black and white thought so darkly that instead of making life and death the issue about what knows us and what doesn't we let it all live all the time since we don't know what we'll lose.

ners know when something is dead. Some might say modernity good gardeners know when something is dead. Some might say modernity neglects death. You know what that makes postmodernity.

imagine great gardens at the other end of our plumbing, all the sometimes I imagine great gardens at the other end of our plumbing, all the seeds in plant heaven.

What do we see when we see a plant? Do we even see them anymore? Did we ever see them? What do they look like? This very basic inquiry, this stop-for-a-moment-and-make-sure-we-are-on-the-same-page inquiry, here's an important consideration of Plato's ideal forms. There is a factor generic to plants we can begin to describe, but if described by sight alone it gets complex fast. Taxonomies, then. Yup. And the machine of knowledge is on the prowl.

Can we even imagine telling problems to a plant? Which plant? That plant?

When we think of love

Returning to meeting someone new for the first or second time: the future of our frame will be challenged. They have and can see things we can't. It seems like magic, it seems terrifying, the world is not merely what is our case. We can be taken along by this enchantment. But our own case remains, and neglected can sprout elements that once we return to ourselves either by choice or somethingelse , these parts are foreign to us. Without tending, overrun by what got by on what we left behind.

Those that consider only alternative route of understanding, who give away their ground easily. Who forget the grounds they are able to make the case upon. One taxonomy, those who chart a better or more full, deeply experienced, feeding the spiritual, righting the limitations of outside oppressors, inside oppressors, freeing oneself from the cares of a highly mediated society, finding the light... written works. A guru that emerges in your perception has been fed upon the unmanaged corners of your ground. They look like answers because they were birthed in the problem.

Problems are fed and kept alive by answers. And the answer that we so desperately seek is not the acceptance of only problems. Besides, the battle of problems and answers is only fought from without. That is actually not quite true. That's where we think they are fought, amongst understanding as we see fit. In actuality, whether we believe it or not, we may ask as many questions, present as many problems, but we only ever live the answers. The whole schtick about 'being the change... and so on' is true perhaps. But it temporalizes the schedule of becoming, maybe soon who knows, something you would prefer to be. More accurate would be to say that we already are our vision of a world, pay attention and adjust as needed.

Plants don't have problems. They are shaped and shape.

We must then consider that there are relationships of friendship between us and plants. Dependencies. And a plant may be a plant may be a rose, but our objects are snapshots, postcards of our relationship to plants. To the ground beneath our feet.

We could go a couple of directions here. We could approach the issue of desire's reliance on the lit individual. We could consider extrasensory perception. Abolishing the veracity of the mind reader, a hoax, a sham, a parlour trick. This is the confusion of what constitutes mind. It is possible to pay such close attention that the ground of a person is revealed to another. And we consider this magic. But it is only a paying attention. The people seemingly in charge of what is what, we have put them in power because they are so good at making us feel safe, of tucking us in with bedtime stories of walls.

But this in itself is a bedtime story, placing a boundary between our naive selves and those we might trust to know better, that create our garden plot. A long time ago, as is often the case with stories we lose track of, reasonings obscured, we stopped believing in magic. But really, we just decided one magic was all the magic we wanted.

What we find odd and mysterious is misplaced. When we see a photon do more than one thing at the same time, we use our understanding of waves, fields, but we also see the photon. We exclaim how odd it acts. But perhaps the oddity is that we don't have the capacity to explain in our limited curiousity cabinet of words, language, concepts — we are the odd ones.

What can be described can be governed. It truly is not difficult to see how identity politics, how liberal inclusion works to benefit the governors.

We turn away from the magics of emotion, intuition, we consider dangerous what we can't explain, can't name. Only within stories in which this dark place serves the light do we acknowledge its fecundity.

Try to attempt a definition of what love is.

Love at first sight only exists in the history of its survivors.

"What you feel before you feel something you've never felt before."

Philosophy as the practice of the wisdom of love, as the fearless encounter with an opening beyond. We can only live what we are unable to perceive. There is no end. Sorry to break it to you. Certain traditions may perish, we are certainly at the end of our rope in considering merely the application of sight as the path to Knowledge, oops. Without crop rotation, fields once rich become depleted. That is not, I repeat not to say we should never plant soy beans again. Just that not every spring. Knowledge is practice. But again! The polemic drawn here is not the contradiction against knowledge as accumulated pieces of somesuch. The polemic attempted is against the very impossibility in a certain framework that both can't be true. And yet we let photons be more than one thing and expect the product of their illumination to reduce the complications instead of 1) remain as complicated as they are (whether we yet understand the depth of said complications) or 2) to increase the complications as long as deep as wide as long.

Our minds do so much work to adjust the world so that it makes sense, so we can move in space, understand our orientation to said space, and interact. It makes invisible the frames, a courtesy, really. It does not demand our ignorance. Spin around fifty times real fast. Many of the experiments we engage with that push the boundaries of our invisible sensory framework are fun. Probably for good reason.

Philosophy is a practice that yields concepts. But not unlike farming, the crops must be harvested. There is no point to a farmer who plants without reaping. And of course, the spoils move on - with or without heavy processing, exportation, exploitation. We can mention theory at this point, the lovely cook.

The author lives and works in México City. Cheerfully discontent with a reasonable trajectory of graduate scholarship, she fosters a professional career as a craft bartender and culinarian while engaging in her work as writer and editor.

She holds an AAS in Culinary Arts & Management from Le Cordon Bleu, MPLS; a BA in Communicative Production, a self-designed degree from University of Minnesota; an MA in Media Philosophy from The European Graduate School, Saas-Fee Switzerland; and is currently completing her Ph.D at EGS as well, her dissertation work investigating ethical inquiry on the playing field of what could be considered micropolitics.

There are scholastic performances, projects, and editorships to be found by any basic web search, as well as ancient silly photos and artwork, mostly random postcards which the author still engages oneself.

She is also famous for her fried chicken and biscuits.

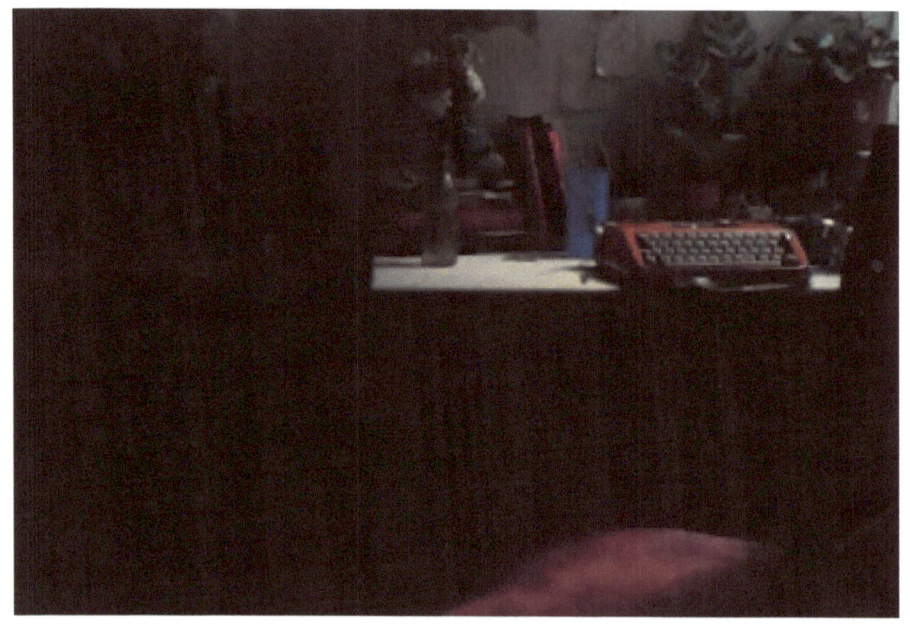